Moving out, Moving on

when a relationship goes wrong workbook

Susan Murphy-Milano

KindLiving Publishing, LLC
1-888-232-3417
www.movingoutmovingon.com

Published by KindLiving Publishing, LLC.

1-888 232-3417 First Edition.

ISBN 0-9764089-0-2

Book Design by Kathryn McBride,
Christine Nelson & Sarah Mehringer

Acknowledgments

No effort of teaching and communication is ever achieved without the guidance and support of those we carefully surround ourselves as we journey on life's delicate road. For me, my journey began when my mother prepared me for a life of helping others. Through her passing, she taught me the true meaning of compassion and love that continues to grow with each new sunrise.

I would first like to acknowledge a profound debt to those at Borders Group, Inc. who worked effortlessly in the completion and ultimate publication of this book.

To David Jungel for setting this entire process into motion and for being its caring shepard. You have made this project a reality.

I am humbled by the kindness and friendship of Robert Consigny, Barbara Hardin and Judge Nancy Sidote Salyers, for agreeing to read and endorse this book. Most with schedules so full it was hard to imagine they'd say yes. Thank you for your generosity and support.

To Kathryn McBride; mother, sister, aunt and someone I'm proud to call my friend. You have stood by me supporting my work on behalf of families near and far. Most of all, you have taught me that God, in his own time, not my time, does answer our prayers. He is with us every step on our journey until we return home to our resting place.

For my son, Vincent, and Step-Daughter, Mary Kathleen; know that you are both loved.

And to my husband Steven, without you I would not have experienced the greatest gifts of all; Love, Light and Laughter. For that I thank you, and I am, at last, at peace.

Table of Contents

Foreword

Ending a relationship is not an easy road to travel. It is survivable if you are willing to do the work necessary to move on with your life. You will make it.

Remember, "Knowledge is Power." Let this book be your guide as you begin your journey from being emotionally stung to personal empowerment!

This workbook will provide you with a road map when you are moving on. It will help you notify your child's school or day care center, financial institutions, your employer, and child support enforcement. It will also help you change the beneficiary on a life insurance policy, and select a lawyer or find other information that is essential to your security.

This workbook will also help you reduce the stress of divorce or ending a live-in relationship. Keeping all your information in one place makes the process easier. The forms in this workbook will enable you to work with creditors and utility companies. All too often, as a person is divorcing or ending a relationship that includes abuse or stalking, the significant other becomes hurt and angry. They may have your utilities shut off, change financial information that would affect your credit, and so on. Because they have access to your personal information such as your birth date and social security number, they could ruin your good credit which could take years to correct. If you've been down this road before, you know that creditors are not sympathetic to any explanation you give them - whether it's the truth or not. The bottom line is that creditors only know that your name appears in their database. You are listed as the responsible party even if the information was changed without your knowledge. This workbook provides you with the remedies to protect yourself - before it is too late. By using these forms, no one will be able to access or change personal information without your knowledge or permission.

Computer technology has become an important part of our everyday lives. Access to your confidential information is now readily available to almost anyone who knows how to use a computer. This workbook will also assist you in protecting your personal information, on computers or the Internet.

Whether you use all of the forms or just a few contained in this workbook, make sure you keep a copy of each document you use for your own records. I have provided a form on page 129 that will allow you to record the information you have sent out if you are not able to make photocopies. It is a good idea to follow-up each letter within ten business days after you have provided your information. Next place a call to confirm that your letter has been received and properly entered in their database. Also, write down the name of the person you spoke with, along with the date and time on the sheets we have provided.

If you wish to use the forms included in the workbook or on the enclosed disk simply as a guide or template, we suggest that you "cut and paste" to create a letter that best fits your needs. Feel free to strike-out any language that does not apply to you. For example, if you do not have children, strike-out the portions of the letters referring to children.

If you're worried about your personal safety, it's a good idea to include your detailed concerns on every form. Also, make sure to provide a detailed explanation of why your information must be kept confidential.

If you have received an order of protection from a judge in either civil or criminal court that prohibits the abuser from coming near you, (and/or your children, relatives, residence, place of employment, etc.) photocopy the court order and attach it to the appropriate letters. Make sure to carry a copy with you.

Remember, only you can protect yourself.

CD Instructions: Enclosed on the CD are forms A-N listed in the workbook. For your convenience, files are in both Microsoft Word and Adobe PDF format and will work on both PC and MAC based computers. Feel free to type your own information into the form or cut and paste information as needed for each individual situation.

This guide provides information with respect to the subject matter covered. No claims or representations are made. Please seek the assistance of a qualified attorney for professional advice in your area. The goal of this guide is to arm you with information regarding your divorce, separation from spouse, friend, or partner. This information will save you money, time, and many headaches. *Moving out, Moving on* is a process that helps you manage and control.

Emotions run high during these conflicts. By following the information provided, you will be able to move through this transition, stronger and more resilient than ever.

I want you to know that I understand that you are probably in a situation that you know little about. This guide will help you regain control and move on to a new life, full of hope and vigor.

A divorce or separation is not always adversarial. Some couples can work together, which saves money, time, and aggravation. Whether your separation is simple or complicated, you will find the information you need in these pages. When you complete this guide, please interview and retain an attorney.

One way to minimize legal costs effectively is to be prepared before you go to an attorney. That means laying out the foundation by knowing what you want before you seek assistance. It is important for you to read the lawyer information worksheet section located on pages 5-7.

Often, finding the right attorney can be time consuming and difficult. Ask friends or relatives for suggestions. In some situations; however, this may not be a good idea. Contact the American Bar Association in your state, listed on pages 81-83. This attorney referral service directs you to attorneys in the area where you live.

THE ROLE OF AN ATTORNEY

When you reach the decision to end the marriage, you will need to contact an attorney. If you are filing for a divorce, or your partner has already sought legal representation and filed papers through the courts for a divorce, you will need to hire a lawyer who specializes in divorce and can properly represent your interests. There are usually obvious signs that your marriage is ending. No one gets out of bed one morning and says, "I think I'll file for divorce today." Consulting with a legal professional before you are served with divorce papers will better prepare you in the days and months that follow. A good attorney will be able to provide you with a clear understanding of your legal rights.

In addition, if there are children involved, a divorce attorney will be able to handle various issues as they relate to the "best interest" of the minor(s). There is information in this book to help you. For example, "Important Questions Regarding Your Children," and a "Temporary Parenting Plan." By going over these questions, you may be able to work out issues with your partner that affect your children prior to hiring an attorney, which will only save you time, money, and possible headaches down the road. If, for some reason, your partner is not willing to sit down with you, do it yourself.

HOW TO HIRE AN ATTORNEY

If you can afford to hire your own attorney, you should choose someone with whom you are comfortable. Remember, the final decision is yours. You can begin by making an appointment for an initial consultation (this is usually free of charge). All communications with the attorney will be confidential, even after you have met with one and decided to hire someone else.

Legal Information *(Continued)*

COMMUNITY PROPERTY STATES

In a community property state, all assets and debts belonging to a married couple, are divided equally between the two parties. Arizona, California, Idaho, Louisiana, New Mexico, Texas, Washington and Wisconsin are states that have community property laws.

REMEMBER: Any debt accumulated during the marriage is also your responsibility, even if you had no say in the expense. So if you are considering a divorce, look at both your assets and debts.

Go to the library or the Internet and research the laws regarding divorce in your state.

CHILD SUPPORT: WHAT CAN YOU EXPECT?

Following a divorce, a woman's standard of living drops by approximately 30 percent over a 5-year period while a man's rises by 8 percent. This is unfair, but a reality. Expect a lifestyle change. Creating two separate households from one will mean a lot less money. So, maybe getting your nails done every week is no longer an expense you can afford. Those little luxuries that you once took for granted may no longer fit into your new lifestyle. If you have been responsible for paying the bills and keeping the checkbook, your significant other will probably believe that you will be fine, and able to care for the kids on two hundred dollars in child support a month.

It might be a good idea to send him a quarterly statement of receipts and expenses so he will have an idea of what is being spent each month. They forget that you are left with the enormous responsibility of paying for food, clothes, a place to live, and education etc.

If you argued about financial matters during the marriage it will be no different for you once you are divorced.

By law, each state has guidelines for the percent of child support that is paid and will depend on how many children you have. A judge determines the amount to be paid based on the other parent's income. The court also determines if child support will be deducted from his paycheck by his employer, sent to a state agency that then forwards it to you, or just sent to you directly.

If you do not have a good relationship with your spouse and extra money has not been approved by the courts or is not part of the approved court settlement, you do not have the right to demand that a spouse pay you additional money if he doesn't want to.

If your spouse loses his job, or is laid off, he most likely can apply for a temporary reduction in child support payments.

BEING PREPARED

It is very important to be prepared prior to meeting for an initial consultation with a potential attorney. The workbook contains monthly expense forms and distribution of personal property forms that you should review in order to have a greater understanding of your personal finances and what you will need to live on once the divorce is final. This information should not be disclosed to an attorney until you have selected legal representation. Get yourself a legal pad and write down a list of questions to ask before you meet with the attorney.

Lawyer Information Worksheet

Here are some suggested questions:
Lawyer's Name, phone number, and address:

_____

_____

_____

_____

1. Where did you (the lawyer) attend law school?

_____

2. How long have you been practicing law?

_____

3. What percentage of your practice is devoted to divorce/family law? (This is very important.)

_____

4. Are you experienced in child custody cases or domestic violence issues* and do you keep current on case law?

_____

5. Can you estimate how many divorce cases you handle a year?

_____

6. Do you inform your clients immediately when complications arise and about strategies you would like to use as a case proceeds?

_____

If you have been in an abusive marriage you should inquire as to the lawyer's expertise as it relates to domestic violence, orders of protection, stalking, and whether or not he has represented women who have been abused.

FINANCIAL QUESTIONS TO ASK

Attorneys charge in one of three ways: an hourly rate, flat fee, or on a contingency fee basis. You could begin by asking:

1. What is your (the lawyer) hourly rate?
    a. for office time?_____
    b. for court time? _____

2. What kind of fee arrangements are available?

_____

3. What is your billing rate for telephone calls to clients or others involved in a case?

_____

4. Do you charge for copies? _____

5. a. What is included in the hourly rate?

_____

    b. What is excluded in the hourly rate?

_____

6. Do you require an up front retainer fee for services?

_____

7. Will you be handling my case or will I be dealing with others such as a paralegal or law clerk?

_____

8. If others are working on my case, such as non-lawyers or others from your office, what hourly rate will I be charged?

_____

9. Are you familiar with the tax laws regarding divorce settlements?

_____

Lawyer Information Worksheet (Continued)

10. Based on the current state laws, what am I entitled to as it relates to property, child support, pension, monthly maintenance, etc.?

_____

11. Will an itemized bill for your services be sent on a monthly basis?

_____

12. Are there additional fees for the following services?

   a. settlement negotiations_____

   b. preparing for trial_____

   c. conference with experts_____

   d. conference with other lawyers_____

Important Tips

- You should interview at least 3 different lawyers before you make a decision.
- Dress neatly and business-like. Do not wear a lot of makeup and do not chew gum or candy.
- Don't be nervous. You are there to interview them, not to be interviewed.
- After each interview take a few minutes to write down your thoughts and your comfort level. The key is, did they answer all your questions?
- It's very important not to hire a lawyer based on looks or reputation alone. Can they get the job done for you? That is the question you need to ask.
- Whatever you do, leave your money, checkbook, and credit cards at home until you have made a clear decision.

Handing the potential lawyer a personal information sheet will save you some time. Either retype the following information or neatly hand write the form. This saves time in the interview, because most lawyers only allow 30 to 45 minutes for an initial interview.

Date:

_____

Name, phone number, and address:

_____
_____
_____
_____

Age:_____

Years married:_____

Date, county, and state of marriage:

_____

Employed by:

_____
_____

Years worked:_____

❑ I do not work outside the home

Spouse's name, phone number, and address:

_____
_____
_____
_____

Spouse's age:_____

Spouse's employer:

_____
_____

Years worked:_____

❑ Spouse does not work outside the home
❑ Own our own home
❑ Rent our home
❑ Live with relatives

The number of children from this marriage is:____

Name, age, and birth date:

_____

Name, age, and birth date:

_____

Name, age, and birth date:

_____

(List all children)

Lawyer Information Worksheet *(continued)*

Once you have selected a lawyer, write down his contact information in the space below.

Name of Law Firm	*Name of Lawyer*
Address	*Telephone Number*
Email	*Name of Assistant*

RETAINER AGREEMENT *(Example on page 9)*
Once you have decided on the attorney who will represent you, ask for a retainer agreement from them so that you know what is expected of you as the client. Do not allow anyone to intimidate you in this process. If you do not understand something that is said or given to you in writing, ask, ask, ask!

I _____ retain Attorney_____to
(*Your name*)   (*Attorney's name*)

represent me in the following family law matter:

Divorce from _____.
(*Name of Spouse*)

I understand and agree that I am retaining Attorney_____
(*Attorney's name*)
and he/she is accepting employment on the following terms and conditions:

This agreement becomes effective when Attorney _____ receives
a signed copy of the Retainer Agreement and a retainer in the amount of $_____, plus
an additional $_____ for expenses. If the retainer is depleted or it becomes apparent
that the retainer will be depleted, I agree to pay an additional retainer or work out a satisfactory payment plan to supplement the retainer. Any portion of the retainer not used to pay costs or earned
earned attorney fees is refundable.

All services performed by Attorney _____ will be billed at the rate of
$_____ per hour. I will be charged for all time spent by Attorney_____
on this case, including telephone calls to and from Attorney _____, office
conferences, sending or receiving correspondences, documents, drafting, research, court appearances, and any other time spent by Attorney _____ on my case.

In addition to attorney's fees, I will pay Attorney _____ for necessary out-
of-pocket costs including, but not limited to, deposition expenses, service-of-process expenses, filing
fees, witness fees, travel expenses, reporter fees, and investigative expenses. Attorney
_____ may request that I pay large out-of-pocket costs directly, and I will
consent only after reviewing either in person or by mail a list of those costs that are to be deemed
out of pocket.

I appoint Attorney _____ as my agent and authorize Attorney _____
to hire experts only with my knowledge and prior approval and make advances to those experts on
my behalf, although I am liable for all expert fees, costs, and expenses. If convenient, Attorney
_____ may arrange for me to enter into independent fee agreements with those
experts.

Attorney _____ will send monthly billing statements to me. I will
promptly pay any balance due on those statements unless otherwise agreed. I understand that the
total fees earned may be greater than the retainer.

When Attorney _____ completes this matter, I will receive a final
statement showing the balance due, if any, for legal services rendered and costs advanced. I agree
to pay the balance due on the invoice labeled "Final Statement" within 30 days from when I receive it
unless otherwise agreed. If I do not pay the balance due by then, my account will be considered past
due, and a past-due charge of 12% per year (1% per month) will be added to the outstanding balance and compounded monthly until the bill is paid in full.

Example of Retainer Agreement

Attorney _____ may withdraw from representing me if I do not pay my bills or give other security to Attorney _____ for the payment of his fees; if I misrepresent or fail to disclose important facts; if I fail to follow Attorney _____ advice; or if I fail to provide necessary information or otherwise fail to cooperate with Attorney_____.

I have the right to discharge Attorney _____ for any reason at any time. If I do so, Attorney _____ will withdraw from representing me.

If Attorney _____ withdraws, I remain responsible for all fees, costs, and expenses actually incurred under this agreement. I will either make payment in full or give other security acceptable to Attorney_____. Attorney _____ will return my documents to me.

I authorize Attorney _____ to perform all services that Attorney _____ believes are necessary to this representation, including negotiating the settlement of any or all issues with the opposing attorney or opposing party if no attorney has been hired. However, no settlement will be finalized without my consent.

I acknowledge that Attorney _____ has made no promises or guarantees concerning the outcome of this action.

This agreement for services applies to my divorce at the trial court. Any appeal will be handled by Attorney _____ only at my specific request and with Attorney _____ consent. I will be advised at that time of the probable charges for such an appeal.

Storage of Files: I understand that due to space limitations, it is firm policy that files be stored in your storage area for five years after the conclusion of a particular matter. After five years, the file is destroyed. If I should desire a copy of the file or any part of it after the conclusion of the matter, it will be my responsibility to make a specific written request for those documents. If no such request is made, the file will be destroyed after five years in accordance with firm policy.

Increase of hourly rate: I understand that Attorney _____ hourly rate may increase by up to ten dollars per hour on January 1st of each year. If Attorney _____ hourly rate increases after January 1st, I agree to pay the new hourly rate for all work done by Attorney _____ after January 1st.

I HAVE READ AND UNDERSTAND THIS AGREEMENT, AND I AGREE TO BE BOUND BY ITS TERMS.

Dated this _____ day of _____, 20____

Approved:

_____ Law Office   By:_____

Moving Out, Moving On

11

Moving Out, Moving On

WHEN A DIVORCE IS UNEXPECTED

Sometimes there are no warning signs or notice given to prepare for the fateful day when you are told, "I don't love you anymore." Your first reaction may be devastation. You thought you had it all. Why, and when, did this happen? Unfortunately, after the shock wears off, you end up being controlled by your emotions. This can be very dangerous. You must get ahold of yourself no matter how you are feeling.

Follow these steps to keep on track:

- Consult a lawyer immediately (consultation for the first hour is usually free).
- Bring with you to the lawyer a list of prepared questions to ask (see list provided on page 5-8).
- Try not to spend that free hour crying or talking about your marriage. A lawyer is not there to be your therapist. Stick to the facts. You are there to interview and possibly hire him.
- Copy all documents including wills, car titles, etc., and anything you find on the computer (see list provided).
- If you have a video camera or camera, take two pictures of everything including appliances, cars, artwork, antiques, jewelry, furniture etc.
- Whatever you do, do not move out until the divorce is final (consult a lawyer first).
- If you have never had a credit card in your own name, start applying now to establish a credit history of your own.
- Try to remain as calm as possible when you tell the children. Do not speak negatively of, or badmouth the other parent.
- Do not use your children as a confidant. Do not involve your children in divorce preparation.
- Try to keep the kid's regularly scheduled activities and routines as normal as possible.

IN A DIVORCE WHO DECIDES?

What is acquired during the marriage is considered marital property. For example, if you bought your home during your marriage and your name is not listed with your spouse on the deed it is still marital property. The court, not you, your spouse, or a lawyer, decides what is fair. It is also your responsibility to prove what assets exist. For example, if you know your spouse has liquidated assets, it is up to you to provide proof of this to a judge. If you are successful, a court may award you an amount equal to the value that your spouse liquidated.

MARITAL SETTLEMENT AGREEMENT

The Marital Settlement Agreement is very important. It is usually drawn up by the lawyer of the person who filed for the divorce. For example, if you filed, then you are listed on the court documents as the petitioner and your spouse is listed on the court documents as the respondent.

The Marital Settlement Agreement contains the final terms of the agreement by both you and your spouse. It may include:
- Custody placement of the minor child (children)
- Maintaining a residence in that state and prohibiting the child's (or children's) removal from the state without the consent of the court, including taking the minor child (or children) for vacations out-of-state
- Visitation by the other spouse
- The child's (children's) school placement
- The amount of child support to be paid monthly, and when support payments end
- It may include college tuition expenses
- It must include that you receive a current or active copy of a life insurance policy naming the child (or children) as beneficiary (or beneficiaries) with an amount agreed upon by both parties
- Medical and health care expenses

PROPERTY DIVISION
• Division of financial assets listing who will receive what and how much
• A detailed list of household items and the distribution of items
• Debts and financial obligations and who is responsible for them after the divorce is final
• This includes or should include taxes

DIVORCING AND YOUR CREDIT
It is a nice thought to be able to wipe the slate clean and allow us to clear our personal credit history when we divorce, but that is not how it works.

When you divorce, your partner may be ordered by a judge to pay joint debts, such as credit cards, car payments, loans, mortgages, etc. and it may say in your divorce decree that you are not responsible for certain financial obligations that were created while you were married. However, in the eyes of creditors; you and your credit history are still responsible until the debt has been paid off completely.

Take for example: You bought two cars during your marriage and the loan is in both your names. During your divorce it's agreed that you and your spouse will each take a car and be responsible for the loans on the vehicle you will be taking. You are still responsible for the payments on both cars and your credit will be affected if payments are late or your partner has filed for bankruptcy. If that happens, it will have a negative impact on your ability to secure future financing, and may cost you additional interest and fees because you were listed with bad credit, even though your partner was "responsible" for the loan. To avoid this, consider refinancing the loans in each of your names while you are still legally married.

Talk with your lawyer about your financial responsibilities when it comes to joint debt from the marriage. (See Credit Report Request on page 79.)

THE IMPORTANCE OF UNDERSTANDING INSURANCE
You may not be aware that insurance companies use credit-based scoring to determine the insurance premium you are charged for insurance. You are rated on a credit score much like a loan or a credit card application.

Here are some things in your credit history, which may affect your insurance score:
• The number and type of credit card accounts (both jointly and individually)
• The length of time the account has been open
• Whether payments were on time or late
• Any money judgments against you
• Whether you ever filed bankruptcy
• The number of years you have had a credit history

You are given a Financial Rating Code (also known as FRC), which is determined from your insurance score. The score points range from 1 thru 10 with 10 being assigned the highest discount.

When getting insurance quotes for your home, car, health, or business, always ask what your (FRC) rating. This is one of the many factors that is used in developing your insurance premium. It is in your best interest to check your credit history every year if for no other reason than to make sure your insurance premiums are at the lowest rate possible.

Ask the Insurance Agent what your FRC is. If they tell you, "it was not as good as it should be," ask what credit bureau they used to obtain your credit information. Then, write the credit bureau and ask that you receive a free copy of your credit report by stating you received an "Adverse Action Notice." This needs to be done within 60 days.

Moving Out, Moving On *(continued)*

-Information obtained for insurance scoring is supposed to be kept confidential. They are not allowed to release this, or any information, without first getting your permission.

IMPORTANT NOTE: The score received is not used to determine your eligibility for insurance, but rather the rate you pay.

It is important for you to review all insurance polices. Sit down with an insurance agent and have him explain your current policies and what you need, or don't need, as you move forward.

Get insurance quotes from three (3) different sources and compare the rates and coverage. When you have made a decision, make sure you are able to handle the premiums.

When divorcing, ask your agent to provide you with a change of beneficiary form for your life insurance policy.

Never cancel a current policy. In many situations, you can keep your policy and have the agent make changes to the one you already have. Replacing insurance may cost you a lot more money. Have a licensed insurance agent (not a secretary or friend) explain and help you keep, replace, or change insurance.

If you need to refinance your home, rental, or vacation property, make sure you have listed in your policy any changes you made during the refinancing such as a new bank lender who secured the loan. Just look under "Secured Interest Parties" to see if a new lender needs to be listed on the insurance policy. (Not having insurance coverage is in direct violation of your lending agreement, therefore you need another plan if you are not able to afford the insurance premiums.)

When filling out an insurance application, be sure to review and complete each section carefully before you sign and submit the document.

Make sure that you review your policies every couple of years with a licensed insurance agent.

VEHICLE MAINTENANCE
Remember to take your car in for oil changes and repairs as needed. Have the tires, plugs, belts, and battery checked. Go to someone you can trust to keep your car in top working condition.

When creating a legal document of any type, always make sure to have it reviewed by a lawyer or certified financial estate planner.

WILLS

A will is an important document created by you in order to guarantee that your assets are distributed to those you select after your death. Be sure to change this document when you divorce and be sure to review it periodically. Also, remember to change beneficiaries on life insurance or retirement accounts. If you are going to create a will yourself, without the help of a lawyer, make sure you research and follow the correct guidelines in your state.

ADVANCE HEALTH CARE DIRECTIVE

You can prepare an advance health care directive on your own. These forms are usually available at your doctor's office, hospital, or local office supply store. This is very important to have with your personal papers and should be placed in your personal medical file. Should you become seriously ill or are unable to speak for yourself, this allows you to appoint and/or give instructions to someone you trust with regard to your medical care.

POWER OF ATTORNEY

A power of attorney is a legal document that gives someone you choose, legal permission to handle all your personal and financial matters in the event you cannot. It's a good idea to prepare an agreement first, in draft form, and then take it to a lawyer for review.

WHAT IS A LIVING TRUST

A living trust is a trust you create while you are alive that holds ownership to your assets during your lifetime. You as the grantor, fund the trust with such things as stock certificates, property you own, bank accounts, etc. You are also able to buy and sell assets in your trust while still alive. A living trust avoids your estate from going into probate and transferring assets after your death.

When considering divorce, or, if you have been taken by surprise and your spouse served you with divorce papers, what is the first thought that comes to your mind? I need to get a lawyer! Why don't we ever think of other alternatives like mediation?

What is a mediator? It is a neutral person. They do not take sides and they are not there to be your marriage therapist. Their goal is to assist you by removing the tension and drama often associated with a long drawn out bitter court battle. In fact, they are not even allowed to give legal advice. The mediator meets with each of you separately. You fill out questions and provide financial information. In addition, you list concerns over custody and parenting issues.

You will then meet with the mediator together and work out the issues so that you can come up with an agreement that serves you both. That agreement is then submitted to the courts for final review usually by a judge. (States vary on this, so please check your local statutes.)

The goal of mediation is to not place any blame in the marriage, but rather promote and plan for a healthy future for you, your spouse, and your children. You create the divorce agreement between the two of you with the assistance of the mediator and not the courts.

Before you say, "I am not interested in doing that, I want to hire a lawyer," you should seek consultation with a lawyer to understand your options. A lawyer can review the documents drawn up by a mediator and make changes and suggestions before it is submitted to the courts.

Have you ever sat in on a divorce case or trial? The answer most likely is no. Before you make that all important life-changing decision, why don't you go to your local courthouse to family court or domestic relations (whatever it may be called in your area) and sit through a morning or afternoon of court calls and/or hearings of others going through a divorce. It is not a pretty sight, especially if there is a lot of tension between the divorcing parties, the lawyers, and the judge. As you view the court process, try to picture yourself sitting there with your lawyer and your spouse sitting with his lawyer. Observe the fact that these two intelligent people have hired complete strangers to argue what can become "unimportant stuff" and a court reporter is taking down every word said for the court that will then become public record. Do you really want to participate in ending your marriage that way? Some of those people in court have been there for a year or more and still are not divorced. Why? Because they could not resolve their own issues during their marriage. They are stubborn, angry, or want revenge. In the end, it is the judge-another stranger-who will decide the final outcome of who gets what and when you and your former spouse may see the children. You ultimately DO NOT get to decide.

MEDIATION	vs.	HIRING A LAWYER
• Costs a fraction of what you would pay in legal fees. • Comprises of usually 5-9 visits (will be more or less depending on your situation). • Very private and confidential.		• Retainer fee up front: $2,000 to $5,000 (depending on where you live). • Once the retainer is spent, lawyers begin billing rates of approximately $125 to $450 per hour. • Outside expenses, such as paid experts, depositions, research, copying, conferences with lawyer, court, preparing for trial, etc. begin. • Decision made for you by lawyers and the Judge. • Recorded in a public court record.

YOU CAN HIRE A LAWYER TO MEDIATE YOUR DIVORCE

Many lawyers now offer Divorce Mediation as part of their services. They, however, are not allowed to give legal advice. They are bound by the same rules, to remain neutral in the process, as are mediators who are not lawyers. They can also help you draw up agreements for custody, parenting etc. and the fee for this service is less than the hourly attorney rates.

HIRING A QUALIFIED MEDIATOR

• Call your local Clerks office and ask for a list of mediators in your area.
• Check the yellow pages under Divorce Mediation.
• Make sure whomever you choose has been mediating this for at least 3 years.
• Ask for a list of references.
• Ask for a fee agreement in writing once you have selected someone.
• Consult a lawyer during this process if you are unsure about something.
• Consult with a lawyer before an agreement is finalized to have him review and make any changes to the agreement.

WHAT IS SUMMARY DISSOLUTION OF MARRIAGE?

States such as California, Colorado, Indiana, Minnesota, Nevada, and Oregon allow you and your spouse to bypass the court system completely. In the states mentioned, divorcing couples complete and file a form. The documents you complete must still be filed with the Clerk of the Courts. This form of divorce is legal and binding. In this process, the decision makers are you and your spouse and it's finalized in 21 days. (Check your state laws.)

WHAT IS SIMPLIFIED DIVORCE?

After filing the necessary paperwork and with the assistance of the Clerks Office located in the court house, you both appear in court in order to finalize what both of you have agreed upon. To qualify for this, you cannot have children under the age of 18 or be pregnant. Ask for a booklet at the Clerk of the Courts office to review and use as your guide. The States already doing this are Alaska, Arizona, Connecticut, Florida, Ohio, Tennessee, Washington, and Wisconsin.

Questions Regarding Your Children

Often, as parents, we believe that everything we do has our children's best interest at heart. However, during the most heated time of the separation or divorce, feeling hurt, angry, or rejected often takes center stage in your life and sometimes the children can be caught in the middle. Remember, the children are not getting divorced or separated, you are. It's important that you show your child love and attention. Make sure he doesn't feel he is the cause of the divorce, separation, or breakup.

There is a program for children who are from divorced families called "*Rainbows*" and it is offered to school-age-children in many schools across the country. Please ask the social worker or teacher at your child's school for information on enrollment. It will help him deal with his fears, feelings, and concerns that he may not be able or is unwilling to share with his parents.

It is very important during this time that you do not negotiate anything involving your divorce in front of the children. Also, do not put them in the middle to send messages back and forth to the other parent. Instead, speak with the other parent in person or send a hand-written note. Do not share or discuss your emotional pain with them, instead go and seek professional counseling or a support group for yourself.

We suggest that you take the time and carefully go through each question answering them as realistically as you can. This exercise is important for you, your children, and your attorney.

1. Do I want the child (children) to be with me or the other parent?

_____
_____
_____

2. Do I plan to keep them away from the other parent, or do I feel that it is important to keep lines of communication open so that the child (children) will have a relationship with the other parent?

_____
_____
_____

3. Should a schedule be worked out? (are children to be with mom/dad specified times during the week/weekend, if so how often and when?)

_____
_____
_____

4. If I am unable to be with the children during specified times, do I exchange times and work something out with the other parent, or do I assume responsibility

by providing care via a babysitter, relatives, or other responsible adult?

_____
_____
_____

5. What happens when the children are sick? (Write out options, how you will deal with this situation.)

_____
_____

6. When the children have activities such as sports, ballet, camp, etc., who will take them?

_____
_____
_____

7. What is the information we need to exchange regarding the children's school? How and when will this information be exchanged? If private school, how will tuition be paid?

_____
_____
_____

Questions Regarding Your Children (continued)

8. Are there any restrictions regarding involvement of grandparents? Step-parents or others?

_____
_____
_____

9. How will child/parent telephone communication be handled? How do you feel about sticking to a schedule regarding phone contact?

_____
_____
_____

10. Are there any restrictions on relocating out of State/Country?

_____
_____
_____

11. What will be the involvement with the other parent concerning child's (children's) doctor, dentist, religious training, counselor, and or extra curricular activities?

_____
_____
_____

12. Issues and concerns regarding child's (children's) vacation. What are the restrictions or rules?

_____
_____
_____

13. Should I make arrangements for the child (children) to go to counseling, if so how often, when, and who will pay for this?

_____
_____
_____

14. Who should provide insurance for the child (children)?

_____
_____
_____

15. Should any arrangements be made for the children's college education?

_____
_____
_____

16. What about me? What are my desires as a person regarding work, social activity, and education?

_____
_____
_____

17. Other concerns that I have:

_____
_____
_____

There will certainly be changes and you will need to be more organized. Begin by writing out a detailed schedule. Include taking the children to school, after-school care, activities, getting to work, shopping, meals, laundry, and create an emergency back-up plan.

Some parents prefer to alternate major holidays, some prefer to divide them equally, and some prefer to leave certain days open and flexible to be mutually arranged prior to the event. Holidays and special occasions take priority, no matter which parent the child lives with, and no matter what the regular time sharing schedule will be. Write out your thoughts and include times.

Mother's Day: _____

Father's Day:_____

Mother's Birthday:_____

Father's Birthday:_____

Child's Birthday:_____

Easter: _____

Memorial Day:_____

Independence Day:_____

Labor Day:_____

Halloween:_____

Thanksgiving:_____

Christmas Eve:_____

Christmas Day:_____

Passover:_____

Yom Kippur:_____

Rosh Hashanah:_____

Spring Break: _____

Family Gatherings:_____

Other:_____

Other:_____

Other:_____

Temporary Parenting Plan

By _____   _____
               (Father)   *(Mother)*

for their child (children): Name _____ Age _____

Name _____ Age _____

Name _____ Age _____

Name _____ Age _____

Mother: _____ and Father: _____, in their effort to
have both parents actively involved in their child's (children's) life, have agreed to the following
Temporary Parenting Plan:

1. The couple will continue to share Joint Legal Custody.

2. The primary residence of the child (children) will be with _____
                                                                                    Mother/Father (name one)

3. Time share with mother will be as follows:_____

_____

_____

4. Time share with father will be as follows:_____

_____

_____

5. This plan shall be in effect from _____ until _____.

6. The parents will make every effort to keep within the time frames outlined in this agreement. If there
is going to be a delay of more than 15 minutes, each parent will call the other to alert them of the delay.

7. Pick up of the children will be the responsibility of _____ at the home

of _____. Return of the children will be the responsibility

of _____ at the home of _____.

8. Both parents agree that the other parent should be notified as soon as possible in the event of an
emergency.

9. Neither parent has permission to leave the state with the child (children) without the express written
permission of the other parent. Permission to leave the state with the child, or permission to unilater-
ally change this visitation agreement is not allowable under this plan.

_____   _____
              Signature of Father   *Date*

_____   _____
              Signature of Mother   *Date*

Rent   _____
Mortgage   _____
Electric   _____
Gas   _____
Garbage Service   _____
Water   _____
Telephone   _____
Internet Service   _____
Cable TV Service   _____
Cell Phone   _____   Sub Total_____

Homeowners Insurance   _____
Real Estate Taxes   _____
Other   _____   Sub Total_____

Car Payment   _____
Car Insurance   _____
Car Repairs   _____
Gasoline   _____   Sub Total_____

Food   _____
Clothing   _____
Entertainment   _____
Credit Cards   _____
Childcare   _____
Dependent Care   _____
Tuition   _____   Sub Total_____

Health Insurance   _____
Disability Insurance   _____
Life Insurance   _____
Doctor   _____
Dentist/Orthodontist   _____
Eyeglasses   _____
Medicine   _____   Sub Total_____

Dry Cleaning   _____
Household Help   _____
Beauty Salon/Barber   _____
Pets/Vets   _____   Sub Total_____

Monthly Expenses

Subscriptions _____

Religious Org./Donations _____

Children's Activities _____   Sub Total_____

Accountant _____

Professional Dues _____

Professional Counseling _____

Child (Children) Counseling _____   Sub Total_____
(active/anticipated)

Other: (please list)

_____

_____

_____

_____

_____

_____

_____

_____   Sub Total_____

Monthly Total_____

*If yours is an amicable situation, this form should be submitted to your attorney by both parties. If not, filling out this form and providing to your attorney will save you time and money.

Assets:
  Checking Accounts _____
  Savings Accounts _____
  Certificates of Deposit _____
  Stocks _____
  Bonds _____
  Mutual Funds _____
  Life Insurance Cash Value _____
  Other: _____   Sub Total_____
Investment Assets:
  Real Estate Income _____
  Annuities _____
  Business Interest Income _____
  Partnerships _____
  Other: _____   Sub Total _____
Personal Assets:
  Automobiles _____
  Household Goods _____
  Recreational Vehicles _____
  Collections _____
  Jewelry, Furs, etc. _____
  Trust Funds _____
  Other: _____   Sub Total_____

TOTAL ASSETS_____

LIABILITIES:
  Home Mortgage _____
  Second Home Mortgage _____
  Other Mortgages _____
  Automobile Loans _____
  Loans against Life Insurance _____
  Notes and Trust Deeds _____
  Taxes Due _____
  Credit Cards _____
  Personal Loans _____
  Student Loans _____
  Bills Due _____
  Other: _____

TOTAL LIABILITIES_____

TOTAL NET WORTH_____

(Subtract Liabilities from Assets to reach your total net worth.)

Asset Management *(continued)*

ASSETS:

Home:	❑ Split	❑ Party #1	❑ Party #2
Second Home:	❑ Split	❑ Party #1	❑ Party #2
Automobile #1:	❑ Split	❑ Party #1	❑ Party #2
Automobile #2:	❑ Split	❑ Party #1	❑ Party #2
Checking Account #1:	❑ Split	❑ Party #1	❑ Party #2
Checking Account #2:	❑ Split	❑ Party #1	❑ Party #2
Savings Account #1:	❑ Split	❑ Party #1	❑ Party #2
Savings Account #2:	❑ Split	❑ Party #1	❑ Party #2
Stocks/Bonds/Mutual Funds:	❑ Split	❑ Party #1	❑ Party #2
Pensions:	❑ Split	❑ Party #1	❑ Party #2
Home Furnishings:**	❑ Split	❑ Party #1	❑ Party #2
Collections:	❑ Split	❑ Party #1	❑ Party #2
Businesses:	❑ Split	❑ Party #1	❑ Party #2
Trusts/401K's/IRA's:	❑ Split	❑ Party #1	❑ Party #2
Inheritances Anticipated:	❑ Split	❑ Party #1	❑ Party #2

LIABILITIES:

Home Mortgage:	❑ Split	❑ Party #1	❑ Party #2
Second Home Mortgage:	❑ Split	❑ Party #1	❑ Party #2
Other Mortgages:	❑ Split	❑ Party #1	❑ Party #2
Automobile Loans:	❑ Split	❑ Party #1	❑ Party #2
Loans against Life Insurance:	❑ Split	❑ Party #1	❑ Party #2
Notes and Trust Deeds:	❑ Split	❑ Party #1	❑ Party #2
Taxes Due:	❑ Split	❑ Party #1	❑ Party #2
Credit Cards:	❑ Split	❑ Party #1	❑ Party #2
Personal Loans:	❑ Split	❑ Party #1	❑ Party #2
Student Loans:	❑ Split	❑ Party #1	❑ Party #2
Bills Due:	❑ Split	❑ Party #1	❑ Party #2
Other:	❑ Split	❑ Party #1	❑ Party #2

_____   _____
Party #1 Signature   *Party #2 Signature*

In amicable situations, this form should be submitted to your attorney, signed by both parties. If not amicable, filling out this form will provide information to your attorney regarding your desires for future settlement discussions, with the opposing attorney.

Attach separate sheet listing in detail home furnishings: i.e., furniture, tools, kitchenware, china, heirlooms, art, coins, clothing, computers, televisions, stereos, etc...

A Safety Deposit Box is a good way to keep important documents, jewelry, appraisals, family treasures, etc., from being lost or destroyed. It is also important to inventory and maintain a list of items in your safety deposit box. If you feel comfortable, a list of these items should be given to a trusted family member or friend. Make sure you do not place the only copy of your will and life insurance papers in this box. Should something happen to you, these important papers will be locked when they are needed the most.

ITEMS IN SAFETY DEPOSIT BOX COULD BE AS FOLLOWS: Please check the following items in your box.

- ❑ Birth Certificates
- ❑ Social Security Cards
- ❑ Family Records
- ❑ Marriage Certificate
- ❑ Divorce Decree
- ❑ Service Records
- ❑ Diplomas
- ❑ Citizenship Papers
- ❑ Adoption Papers
- ❑ Insurance Policies
- ❑ Living Will
- ❑ Will

- ❑ Trust Documents
- ❑ Deeds
- ❑ Bills of Sale
- ❑ Car Titles
- ❑ Income Tax Records
- ❑ Cancelled Checks
- ❑ Contracts
- ❑ Agreements
- ❑ Bank Books
- ❑ Pension Certificates
- ❑ Money Market Certificates
- ❑ Savings Bonds *(include serial no.)*

- ❑ Stock Certificates
- ❑ Rare Coins
- ❑ Rare Stamps
- ❑ Rare Books
- ❑ Valuable Jewelry
- ❑ Household Inventoried Items
- ❑ Mortgages
- ❑ Receipts
- ❑ Leases
- ❑ Corporate Records
- ❑ 401K's/IRA's

Social Security Cards:

Name: _____   Number: _____

Name: _____   Number: _____

Stocks & Bonds:

Company	Shares	Certificate #	Date Purchased	Date Due	Price Cost

Savings Certificates:

Certificate #	Face Amount	% of Interest Payment	Schedule of Maturity

Safety Deposit Box *(continued)*

Insurance Policies:

Policy #	Insured by	Type of Policy	Premium Amount	Beneficiary	Date Due

Mortgages and Deeds

Title Company Name	Certificate Number

Property Deeds	Certificate Number	Location of Property

Legal Documents and Agreements

Jewelry Itemization

Miscellaneous

Each time you log onto the Internet, you are announcing your arrival as though you are visiting a friend. As a consumer and user, you should be very careful when going on-line. Each time you visit a site that asks for personal information, and it doesn't have a privacy policy, SKIP IT! Never fill out information that says "optional." Another way to delete codes that follow you around is to go to a consumer protection site that teaches you how to manage and remove information. The site is www.cookiecentral.com/c_concept.htm

When dealing with companies: go to www.consumer.gov. This site is maintained by the Federal Trade Commission and offers buyers' guides, tips, and links to other useful resources.

To insure your safety from an abuser on the Internet, make sure that if you have an e-mail account that you select a password that no one knows but you. If you receive threatening or harassing e-mail, print it out and save it. Then go to your phone book and look up the telephone number for your local US Attorney's office. Sending this type of e-mail could be a federal offense and this office will be able to provide you with information detailing your options.

Make sure to clear information you've gathered and saved on your computer from a person who knows how to read your computer history cache file. To delete this information, check in the help section of your internet browser.

The Internet is probably your best resource for locating just about anything you need. A brief list has been compiled to make your search a little easier. If you do not have access to a computer, go to your local library or look in the yellow pages. It is essential that when seeking legal advice of any kind, it should be sought from a lawyer. These sites are not a substitute for legal services and should be considered as a resource guide only.

INTERNET
http://disney.go.com/cybersafety/
A resource for parents offering valuable lessons about online safety.

REGISTERED SEX OFFENDER REGISTRY
One of the many benefits of the Internet is that important information is readily available at your fingertips.

Sex offenders are required by law to register their locations regularly with the state. Each state has made this information available to the public via the Internet. These registries are individually listed by state. To find the registry pertinent to you, use this example: do a search for "Illinois Sex Offender Registry." You will find www.isp.state.il.us/sor in the search window. Click into that site and follow directions. You can also find a wealth of information for each state at www.sexcriminals.com.

Stay informed and keep your family safe.

INTERNET LEGAL RESOURCE GUIDE
This site offers: basic agreements, buying and selling, credit and collection, employment, leases and tenancies, loans and borrowing, personal and family, transfers and assignments, business, and much more. www.ilrg.com/gov.html

PARENTS GUIDE TO THE INTERNET
This interactive site is not only for kids, but it provides a menu of resources for parents. www.ed.gov/pubs/parents/internet/sites.html

Identity Theft and Fraud

To reduce or minimize the risk of becoming a victim of identity theft or fraud, there are some basics steps you can take. For starters, just remember the word "SCAM."

S Be *stingy* about giving out your personal information to others unless you have a reason to trust them, regardless of where you are:

At Home

1. Start by adopting a "need to know" approach to your personal data. Your credit card company may need to know your mother's maiden name, so that it can verify your identity when you call to inquire about your account. A person who calls you and says he's from your bank, however, doesn't need to know that information if it's already on file with your bank. The only purpose of such a call is to acquire that information for your personal bank checks-such as your Social Security number or home telephone number-the more personal data you routinely hand out to people who may not need that information.

2. If someone you don't know calls you on the telephone and offers you the chance to receive a "major" credit card, a prize, or other valuable item, but asks you for personal data-such as your Social Security number, credit card number, or expiration date, or mother's maiden name-ask them to send you a written application form.

3. If they won't do it, tell them you're not interested and hang up.

4. If they will, review the application carefully when you receive it and make sure it's going to a company of financial institution that's well-known and reputable. The Better Business Bureau can give you information about businesses that have been the subject of complaints.

On Travel

1. If you're traveling, have your mail held at your local post office, or ask someone you know well and

trust (another family member, a friend, or a neighbor) to collect and hold your mail while you're away.

2. If you have to telephone someone while you're traveling, and need to pass on personal financial information to the person you're calling, don't do it at an open telephone booth where passersby can listen to what you're saying; use a telephone booth where you can close the door, or wait until you're at a private location to call.

C *Check* your financial information regularly, and look for what should be there and what shouldn't:

What Should Be There

1. If you have bank or credit card accounts, you should be receiving monthly statements that list transactions for the most recent month or reporting period.

2. If you're not receiving monthly statements for the accounts you know you have, call the financial institution or credit card company immediately and ask about the statements.

3. If you're told that your statements are being mailed to another address and that someone may be improperly using your accounts you should ask for copies of all statements and debit or charge transactions that have occurred since the last statement you received. Obtaining those copies will help you to work with the financial institution or credit card company to determine whether some or all of those debit or charge transactions are fraudulent.

What Shouldn't Be There

1. If someone has gotten your financial data and made unauthorized debits or charges against your financial accounts, checking your monthly statements carefully may be the quickest way for you to find out. Too many of us give those statements, or the enclosed checks or credit transactions, only a

quick glance, and don't review them closely to make sure there are no unauthorized withdrawals or charges.

2. If someone has managed to get access to your mail or other personal data, and opened any credit cards in your name or taken any funds from your bank account, contact your financial institution or credit card company immediately to report those transactions and to request further action.

A *Ask* periodically for a copy of your credit report.

Your credit report should list all bank and financial accounts under your name, and will provide other indications of whether someone has wrongfully opened or used any accounts in your name.

M *Maintain* careful records of your banking and financial accounts.

Even though financial institutions are required to maintain copies of your checks, debit transactions, and similar transactions for five years, you should retain your monthly statements and checks for at least one year, if not more. If you need to dispute a particular check or transaction, especially if your signature has been forged, your original records will be more immediately accessible and useful to the institutions that you have contacted.

Even if you take all of these steps, it's still possible to become a victim of identity theft. Records containing your personal data (credit card receipts or car rental agreements, for example), may be found by or shared with someone who decides to use your data for fraudulent purposes.

Source: *United States Department of Justice*

Suddenly, you have to move or, you are thinking of moving. The Internet can make this time consuming process somewhat easier. If you know the area or state in which you will be living, it's best to check the local newspapers in that area by going on-line to the classified section. This will give you an idea of rent prices and other useful information. If you do not have access to a computer or you have safety concerns, your local library is a great place to do research. Do your homework. See if renting vs. buying is the better option for you. Here are some things to consider while making your decision.

PERSONAL CREDIT CHECK

You should check your credit report on a yearly basis. A credit report can be obtained for a small fee. By law, credit agencies must send you a complimentary report if you have been denied credit. Here are three credit reporting agencies available.

EXPERIAN (TRW)
800.EXPERIAN
P.O. Box 2104
Allen, TX 75013

EQUIFAX
800.685.1111
(cost if $3-8 for a report)
www.equifax.com

TRANS UNION
800.916.8800
P.O. Box 7000
North Olmstead, Ohio 44070
www.transunion.com

MORTGAGE GUIDE

It is important to shop around and ask questions. Whether you are refinancing, reducing debt, making home improvements, or purchasing a home, being organized through this process will help you tremendously. Lenders want to make the loan. Minor or easily fixed credit issues can be worked out or erased by "conscientious" financial people. Talk to them.

1. Obtain a copy of your credit report (see above). Try to do this at least 3 months prior to obtaining a loan. If there is a problem with your credit, this should give you enough time to either clear it up or provide a good explanation to any lender whose job it is to insure you are a good credit risk.

2. If you are attempting to purchase a home, try to get a pre-approval letter from the lender you select. This indicates to the realtor and the seller that you have been approved to make a purchase for the amount indicated in the letter.

3. When researching for loan rates, find out how long it will take to process your mortgage application from the time you submit the paperwork to the closing of the transaction.

4. Be sure to ask the lender for the mortgage rate schedule.

5. Ask the lender for a written list of charges that you will be expected to pay at the time of closing.

6. A loan application will require you to provide at least the following information:
   - ✓ Bank Account Statements
   - ✓ Student Loans
   - ✓ Credit Card Debt
   - ✓ Car Loans
   - ✓ Child Support Income or Payments
   - ✓ References (Those may include: former landlords, employers, and/or educators.)
   - ✓ Copy of Your Last Six Pay Stubs
   - ✓ W2 forms or Tax Returns

✓ Current Financial Obligations
✓ Financial Statements
✓ Other Assets
✓ All Sources of Current Income

Many lenders will help resolve minor credit problems by incorporating solutions like paying off loans or debts from loan proceeds when they see good income and/or extra equity. Do not be discouraged by past problems related to a divorce. They want to make the loan, so speak freely, openly, and honestly.

In addition, you may want to consider a credit bureau as an additional resource for all of your financial needs.

CONSUMER CREDIT COUNSELING

Consumer Credit Counseling Services is a nonprofit organization providing assistance at NO CHARGE for those who need help with budgeting monthly bills, credit card debt, or if you are facing foreclosure. www.cccs.org

BUYING OF REFINANCING A HOME

For you to receive a loan, certain documents and information will be required. Gather the following items prior to contacting a financial institution:

✓ If you are employed, you'll need W-2's for the last 2 years.
✓ Paycheck stubs for one month.
✓ Copies of your tax return for 2 years.
✓ Copies of your bank statements from each bank for last 3 months.
✓ Copies of all stock and mutual fund accounts for last 3 months.
✓ Copies of any stock certificates you may have in your possession.
✓ Copies of statements from your IRA or 401K accounts.
✓ Copies of income producing trusts or trust assets.

✓ If you are divorced, you will need to provide a stamped copy of your divorce decree and property settlement.
✓ If you filed bankruptcy, provide papers along with all schedules.
✓ If you own rental property, provide copies of current 1 year leases for each property and 2 years' tax returns.
✓ If you have other income such as social security, pension, or disability, provide the documentation.
✓ If you rent, provide name of landlord, address, and phone number (at least 2 years).
✓ If you're not a U.S. citizen, then you must provide a copy of your green card both front and back, or if you're not a permanent resident, then provide a copy of your H-1 or L-1 Visa.

If you are self-employed, provide the following:

✓ 2 years' tax returns including 1040 with all schedules signed and dated
✓ Year-to-date profit and loss statements with balance sheets signed by you and the accountant
✓ 2 years' tax returns signed and dated for any business that you own 25% or more
✓ 2 years' tax returns on a general partnership signed and dated
✓ 2 years' K-1's (from any partnerships)
✓ Life insurance policy

APPLYING FOR A LOAN

1. ***Pre-qualifying:*** This will show your credit history and give some idea as to your borrowing power.

2. ***Application:*** When you are ready, you will complete an application, and be required to provide the documents.

3. ***Processing***
   * A credit check is completed
   * Appraisal of current or potential property is completed
   * A title search is completed
   * Verification of where you are employed is completed
   * Verification of where you live is completed
   * Then, the account document information you provided is verified

4. ***Underwriting***
   * Loan goes to underwriter for approval.
   * Conditions are set for the loan
   * Loan is then approved

5. ***Closing:*** Documents are ready to be signed. It is important at this time that you carefully review the documents, preferably with an attorney. Make certain that the terms of the loan and the interest rate are what you accepted. Also, review the name and address to be sure they are correct.

If you are refinancing your home, federal law requires that you be given 3 days to review all documents before the transaction closes. Then, what is signed goes to the title company. As the buyer, you bring in a cashier's check(s) for the amount(s) required and then sign the documents. The title company then records the deed, mortgage (not the note), and other pertinent documents. You are then given the keys to the property.

Did you know there are lenders on line who can pre-qualify you for a loan?

> www.eloan.com
> www.mortgage.com
> www.loanworks.com
> www.quicken.com

To give you an idea of what you would be paying on a monthly mortgage, one of the best sites on the Internet is www.Interest.com, which calculates the amount that you qualify for should you buy a home. The site also explains how to obtain and understand your credit report and the different types of mortgages that are available.

Fannie Mae Consumer Resource Center will send you information on home buying; call 800.732.6643. Fannie Mae Foundation is a nonprofit organization that assists the home buyer with affordable housing and home ownership www.fanniemae.com/index.jhtml

TIPS WHEN RENTING
Apartment/Duplex/House
• How many bedrooms will I need?
• How many bathrooms?
• What appliances are important i.e. dishwasher, microwave, garbage disposal, gas/electric appliances, washer/dryer (on site or in the unit), air conditioning (central or room unit)?
• Am I you looking for a place with a balcony, patio, or fireplace?
• Will I need additional storage?
• What about parking? Do I need a garage or under ground parking?
• Do I want a place that is handicapped accessible? For example, maybe a friend or a relative that is handicapped will be living, staying, or visiting.
• Do I need a place that accepts pets?

What Does the Area Offer that You Need
• Are you near public transportation (good idea if your car doesn't start)?
• If you have children, how close is the nearest school?
• What about parks or outdoor recreation centers?
• How far do you want to be from the grocery store/shopping center?
• Where is the nearest medical facility?

MAKING CALLS FOR A PLACE TO RENT
When calling to ask about a potential place to rent, consider the following tips:

First, unless you are asked, there is no need to announce to the world that you are suddenly single or going through a bad divorce. It is no one's business but your own. If you are still emotional, or in pain, you might sound like a wounded renter or desperate for a place to live. This indicates to a property owner that you are in a hurry and will take just about anything that is available. Instead, try to say something like I need to be closer to my work or children's school or that you just like the area. **This is important:** when you rent you are required to sign a legal and binding document for one year. When our emotions run high, we are unable to think or SEE

clearly what's in front of us. Finding a place to live will be easier, and with less headaches later, if you are calm and armed with a "road map" of what to look for and what questions to ask. If you have children or pets, it's best not to have them in the room when making calls.

Questions to Ask on the Phone:
• How many bedrooms/bathrooms?
• Are utilities included? For example, heat, electricity, water.
• How is the unit heated? (Electric or Gas)
• What appliances come with the unit?
• Is there air conditioning?
• What floor is the unit on? Is there an elevator?
• Where is the unit located?
• Do you allow pets?
• What is the parking situation? Is there parking in a garage, underground, or on the street? (If street, what are overnight street/snow parking rules?)
• How long is the lease?
• When is it available?
• Is the first and/or last month's rent or a security deposit necessary to move in? (How much is the deposit?)
• If you are renting a house or duplex, ask if there is a basement. Is there a washer/dryer hook-up and who is responsible for the lawn and snow removal? (Is it your cost or theirs?)

If you have decided you want to see the unit, make an appointment during daylight hours so you can see how the building is maintained and if it is clean. It is also a good idea to drive by a day or two before and look at the area you are considering and see if it's right for you.

If you Decide to Look at a Place? Do Not Be Shy:
• Turn on all the water faucets to see if they work.
• Look under the kitchen and bathroom sink to check for leaks.
• Flush all the toilets. Look at the floor for cracks or leaks.
• Run the shower and bathtub to see if they are working properly.

• Look at all the appliances in the kitchen and laundry area.
• Look at the walls or carpet. Are they cracked, damaged, or stained?
• Open every cupboard and closet to see if your things will fit (also look for damage).
• Where are the electrical, cable, and telephone outlets, jacks, and switches?
• Most importantly, listen for sounds such as children screaming, dogs barking, or loud noises from the street that you will have to live with.
• Check that the locks on the door are secure.
• Ask if there is access to a manager and maintenance for the building in case of emergency.
• Check the security measures and lighting in the hallway and outside the building.

You Found a Place Where You Would Like to Rent
After you fill out the required application and are approved, you will be asked to sign a lease.
BEFORE SIGNING A LEASE, READ THROUGH IT VERY CAREFULLY.
• Make sure it states the correct address (with your apartment number) on the lease.
• Make sure that the monthly rent and security amount is correct.
• Check that the proper dates when the rent is due are stated and what the late fees are.
• Make sure it states when the landlord/property manager can enter the property and how much time the lease says they will give you before entering. (If it's an emergency they should attempt to contact you first.)
• When does your lease begin and end? Look for a clause regarding how much notice is required to terminate. Notice is usually given in written form. If your lease ends and you have not renewed, you are then on a month to month with a 30 to 60 day notice that you must give to the landlord in order to terminate the lease. This means you just can't move out even though the lease has ended. You will still be required to give proper notice. Lease notice periods are usually not before the 15th and not later than the last day of the month.

• A lease is a legal contract. What is your liability for rent if you have to leave before the lease ends? (Read through the lease carefully.)
• Check to see if you, as the tenant, have to pay for backed-up plumbing, leaks, carpet cleaning etc.
• Are there any other unusual restrictions? Read the fine print.

If there are terms in the lease with which you disagree, feel free to negotiate with the property owner. Make sure that you, and the landlord, initial any corrections or changes. Take a copy of the signed lease with you. Make two/three copies. Keep one with your important documents and give a copy to a friend or relative. Always make sure you have immediate access to a copy for yourself. Have check numbers, dates, and amounts recorded on the original copies of your lease. It is a good idea to get renter's insurance. You can contact your current agent (life, car, health) for a quote. Damages caused by leaky waterbeds, gas grills, and your guests are your legal responsibility.

WHAT IS RENTER'S INSURANCE AND WHY DO I NEED IT?
If you rent a home, apartment, duplex, or condo, it is important for you to obtain a Renters Insurance Policy. If you experience a fire, flood, theft, or vandalism, having renter's insurance will protect your personal property and pay for other accommodations if the damage is such that you have to stay somewhere temporary until it is repaired. The owner or landlord of the property is not liable for the contents of your residence. That is *your* responsibility. Renter's insurance will also protect you from injury to another person or damage to another person's property if an incident happens on the premises.

This type of policy is an inexpensive way to protect yourself. The best way to get information on a renter's policy is to contact the company with whom you insure your automobile. As always, shop around to other agencies in your area to get the best rate.

TIPS WHEN MOVING

You can pick up a free guide on moving tips from your local post office. If you are moving and do not wish others to learn of your plans, please use caution when using the internet to transact business and contact services. Also, if you require return calls from services or businesses and wish to keep the information confidential, then set up another location (a friend's house for instance) where your messages can be received. For additional tips, you can visit www.amazon.com, your local bookstore, or library to obtain a copy of *Defending Our Lives* written by Susan Murphy-Milano.

This would be a good time to use the forms provided to notify utility and credit cards companies, etc. and place a password on your information as a security precaution. *See forms located on pages 45-79*

SEND CHANGE OF ADDRESS FOR:

❑*Post Office:* give forwarding address.

❑*Charge accounts and credit cards*.

❑*Subscriptions:* notice requires several weeks.

❑*Friends and relatives*.

❑*Banks:* Transfer funds, arrange check-cashing in the new city.

❑*Insurance:* notify new location for coverage including life, health, fire, and auto.

❑*Automobile Registrations:* Transfer of car title registration is necessary, also driver's license, city windshield sticker, and motor club membership.

❑*Utility Companies:* Gas, light, water, telephone, perhaps fuel, get refund of any deposits made; arrange in new town for immediate service.

❑*Route Men:* Laundry, paper boy, change-over of services.

❑*School Records:* Ask for transfer of children's records (keep copies for yourself).

❑*Medical, Dental and Prescription Histories:* Ask doctor and dentist for referrals, transfer needed prescriptions, eye glasses and x-rays.

❑*Church, Club and Civic Organizations:* Transfer memberships, get letter of introduction.

❑*Pets:* Ask about regulations for licenses, vaccinations, tags, etc.

AND DON'T FORGET:

❑Empty Freezer - Plan use of foods.

❑Defrost Freezer - Refrigerator - place charcoal inside to dispel odors.

❑Have appliances serviced for moving; tape drawers/doors shut. Tape cords.

❑Call cable company and/or leave remote antenna equipment.

❑Clean rugs or clothing before moving-have them wrapped.

❑With your moving company, check insurance coverage, packing and unpacking, labor, arrival day, various shipping papers, and method and time of expected payment.

❑Plan for special care needs of infants.

ON MOVING DAY:

❑Carry currency, jewelry and documents yourself or use registered mail.

❑Plan transporting pets - they are poor traveling companions if unhappy.

❑Carry traveler's checks for quick, available funds.

❑Let close friend or relative know route and schedule you will be traveling including overnight stops. Use him/her as a message headquarters.

❑Double check closets, drawers, and shelves to be sure they are empty.

❑Leave all old keys needed by new tenant or owner with agent or realtor.

For your convenience, forms A-N found in the *Moving out, Moving on* workbook can also be found on the enclosed CD. Files are in both Microsoft Word and Adobe PDF format and will work on both PC and MAC based computers. Feel free to type your own information into the form or cut and paste information as needed for each individual situation.

This insurance notification form (Form A) has been created to protect your privacy and/or keep your policy in effect. Sometimes a spouse, or even a boyfriend, may get upset and contact the insurance agency to have your policies cancelled.

With this form, you are in control of your situation.

You should send the form directly to the company from where the policy came. For example, you obtained the insurance from an agent in the state where you live but the primary corporation is listed at another location or in a different state. Call the company first to find out where this notice should be sent and to whom. Then also send a notice to the Insurance Agent who handles the policy.

If possible, try to send the copies by registered mail. This way, if there is a dispute and they say it was never received, you have the returned receipt to prove it was received.

Car Insurance *(Phone Number and Contact Sheet)*

_____   _____   _____
(Name of Insurance Company)   (Type of Policy)   (Policy Number)

_____   _____
(Expiration Date)   (Address, City, State, Zip)

_____   _____   _____
(Name of Agent)   (Phone Number)   (Email)

_____   _____   _____
(Name of Insurance Company)   (Type of Policy)   (Policy Number)

_____   _____
(Expiration Date)   (Address, City, State, Zip)

_____   _____   _____
(Name of Agent)   (Phone Number)   (Email)

_____   _____   _____
(Name of Insurance Company)   (Type of Policy)   (Policy Number)

_____   _____
(Expiration Date)   (Address, City, State, Zip)

_____   _____   _____
(Name of Agent)   (Phone Number)   (Email)

_____   _____   _____
(Name of Insurance Company)   (Type of Policy)   (Policy Number)

_____   _____
(Expiration Date)   (Address, City, State, Zip)

_____   _____   _____
(Name of Agent)   (Phone Number)   (Email)

_____   _____   _____
(Name of Insurance Company)   (Type of Policy)   (Policy Number)

_____   _____
(Expiration Date)   (Address, City, State, Zip)

_____   _____   _____
(Name of Agent)   (Phone Number)   (Email)

*YOU MAY USE THIS FORM TO NOTIFY
YOUR CAR INSURANCE AGENT OR AGENCY.*

Date: _____

To: _____
                    (Name of Company)
Address: _____

City, State, Zip:_____

RE: Policy No. _____

TO WHOM IT MAY CONCERN:

On _____, I spoke with _____ from your office.
         (Date)
Please change your records to reflect the following change of address: _____

_____

where all communications and billing inquiries should be sent as of _____.

In addition, I am requesting that a password of _____ be placed on my account

for personal security reasons. Under no circumstances are you authorized to release information without

first obtaining a password. That includes anyone who might contact you saying they were involved in an

alleged accident with me or another family member. The person calling may be trying to gain access to

my new address or telephone number but for safety reasons, I am requesting my information remain

confidential.

Should you need to contact me, please call _____.
                                         (Number of a friend, attorney or yourself)

I thank you in advance for your assistance.

Sincerely,

_____

In this day and age, people are going on-line to pay their utility bills. If you are moving or changing the service into your name, you need to send this form so that no one else can make changes on the account.

If you are unable to make a change to the current service, try to go on-line with your account information. Even though both names are on the account, you can place a password on it so that the account remains open and access is only given to you.

Use the Utilities Form (Form B) for your gas, electric, water, sewer, telephone, cell phone, pager service, cable, and computer service accounts.

It is a good idea if you are divorcing and have never had utility services in your name, to change them over immediately to establish a credit history. Often, in a divorce, a spouse may call to have services ended or just choose not to pay. With this form in place, which requires a password, no one else will be able to disrupt your service.

Make sure to get the name of the customer service person, with whom you speak regarding your phone service, cell phone, Internet, and cable sources. Add a password to the account and then send the form.

If you have any safety concerns, using this form will prevent anyone from accessing your information to change or close joint accounts.

After a couple of weeks, call the companies to make sure the passwords are in effect. If they don't ask you for your password say to them, "You forgot to ask me my password" and then ask to speak with a supervisor. Explain what happened and ask for that person's name. Re-send a form directly to the supervisor. Try calling again to ensure that the changes were made this time. As always, make sure to keep a copy of all the forms you send and a phone log of with whom you speak and when.

Staple or clip a copy of all returned receipts to this page.

Utilities *(Phone Number and Contact Sheet)*

_____   _____   _____
(Name of Company)   (Phone Number)   (Date)

_____   Follow Up Remarks: _____
(Spoke With)

_____

_____

_____   _____   _____
(Name of Company)   (Phone Number)   (Date)

_____   Follow Up Remarks: _____
(Spoke With)

_____

_____

_____   _____   _____
(Name of Company)   (Phone Number)   (Date)

_____   Follow Up Remarks: _____
(Spoke With)

_____

_____

_____   _____   _____
(Name of Company)   (Phone Number)   (Date)

_____   Follow Up Remarks: _____
(Spoke With)

_____

_____

_____   _____   _____
(Name of Company)   (Phone Number)   (Date)

_____   Follow Up Remarks: _____
(Spoke With)

_____

_____

YOU MAY USE THIS FORM TO NOTIFY YOUR GAS, ELECTRIC, WATER, SEWER,
TELEPHONE, CELLULAR PHONE, PAGER SERVICE, AND CABLE COMPANY.

Date: _____

To: _____
(Name of Company)

Address: _____

City, State, Zip:_____

RE: Account No. _____

TO WHOM IT MAY CONCERN:

On _____, I spoke with _____ from your office.
(Date)

I am requesting effective on _____ that all billing inquiries be sent to the
(Date)

following address: c/o _____

_____

In addition, I am requesting that a password of _____ be placed on my account

for personal security reasons. Under no circumstances are you authorized to release information without

first obtaining a password.

Should you have questions or wish to speak with me directly, I can be reached at the following:

_____   _____   _____
(Daytime)   *(Evening)*   *(Other)*

Thank you in advance for your assistance.

Sincerely,

_____

YOU MAY USE THIS FORM TO NOTIFY YOUR GAS, ELECTRIC, WATER, SEWER, TELEPHONE, CELLULAR PHONE, PAGER SERVICE, AND CABLE COMPANY.

Date: _____

To: _____
            (Name of Company)
Address: _____

City, State, Zip:_____

RE: Account No. _____

TO WHOM IT MAY CONCERN:

On _____, I spoke with _____ from your office.
          (Date)
I am requesting effective on _____ that all billing inquiries be sent to the
                                      (Date)
following address: c/o _____

_____

In addition, I am requesting that a password of _____ be placed on my account

for personal security reasons. Under no circumstances are you authorized to release information without

first obtaining a password.

Should you have questions or wish to speak with me directly, I can be reached at the following:

_____   _____   _____
          (Daytime)   *(Evening)*   *(Other)*

Thank you in advance for your assistance.

Sincerely,

_____

YOU MAY USE THIS FORM TO NOTIFY YOUR GAS, ELECTRIC, WATER, SEWER, TELEPHONE, CELLULAR PHONE, PAGER SERVICE, AND CABLE COMPANY.

Date: _____

To: _____
              (Name of Company)
Address: _____

City, State, Zip:_____

RE: Account No. _____

TO WHOM IT MAY CONCERN:

On _____, I spoke with _____ from your office.
         (Date)
I am requesting effective on _____ that all billing inquiries be sent to the
                  (Date)
following address: c/o _____

_____

In addition, I am requesting that a password of _____ be placed on my account

for personal security reasons. Under no circumstances are you authorized to release information without

first obtaining a password.

Should you have questions or wish to speak with me directly, I can be reached at the following:

_____ _____ _____
      (Daytime)   *(Evening)*   *(Other)*

Thank you in advance for your assistance.

Sincerely,

_____

Often customer service representatives who work at financial institutions happily give out information when the caller gives his address, date of birth, social security number, and mother's maiden name. However, not many use or have created a password that prohibits giving information to a caller unless they provide the password requested by the customer service person.

Placing a password, other than your mother's maiden name, the city in which you were born, date of birth, favorite color, or last four digits of your social security number, will stop others from gaining access to your information.

For example, your spouse is upset and you know he will not make your car payment if you are planning to leave. You want to keep the current payment schedule, but need to change the billing address. What do you do? First, you contact the financial institution, get a supervisor's name, and place a password on all your accounts. Then send Form C via registered mail.

For your own safety:
- *Never send an e-mail as a form of communication to any financial institution.*
- *Never reply to e-mails regarding your accounts, or if asked to update information, place a call directly to the company.*
- *Never supply your social security number on the computer.*

Staple or clip a copy of all returned receipts to this page.

Financial *(Phone Number and Contact Sheet)*

_____   _____   _____
(Name of Company)   (Phone Number)   (Date)
_____   Follow Up Remarks: _____
(Spoke With)
_____
_____

_____   _____   _____
(Name of Company)   (Phone Number)   (Date)
_____   Follow Up Remarks: _____
(Spoke With)
_____
_____

_____   _____   _____
(Name of Company)   (Phone Number)   (Date)
_____   Follow Up Remarks: _____
(Spoke With)
_____
_____

_____   _____   _____
(Name of Company)   (Phone Number)   (Date)
_____   Follow Up Remarks: _____
(Spoke With)
_____
_____

_____   _____   _____
(Name of Company)   (Phone Number)   (Date)
_____   Follow Up Remarks: _____
(Spoke With)
_____
_____

YOU MAY USE THIS FORM TO NOTIFY ANYONE TO WHOM YOU OWE MONEY.
FOR EXAMPLE: STUDENT LOANS, CAR LOANS, AND/OR FINANCE COMPANIES

Date: _____

To: _____
    (Name of Company)

Address: _____

City, State, Zip:_____

RE: Account No. _____

TO WHOM IT MAY CONCERN:

My name is _____ and my address is _____

_____

I am requesting the following information be changed on the above referenced account. Please direct all

future communications to: _____

_____

As an additional precaution, I am requesting that a password of _____ be placed

on my account for personal security reasons. Under no circumstances are you authorized to release

information without first obtaining a password. In the event that you receive a court order asking to

release my records, please contact me before you release this information as it may affect my personal

safety.

Should you wish to contact me I can be reached at:

_____   _____   _____
         (Daytime)   *(Evening)*   *(Other)*

Thank you in advance for your assistance.

Sincerely,

_____

cc: _____
         (Name of your Lawyer)

Accountant

Accountant

Your accountant may do business with both you and your spouse or just you. Maybe you have your own business. In a divorce, things get heated. Making sure your information is not released, without a court order signed by a judge, is the best way to protect your financial history.

Send out this form (Form D) via registered mail. Call back in a couple of weeks during lunch hour when you know the accountant is out of the office. Test the person answering the phone. Ask for a document, something minor, to be faxed to you. Contact the accountant directly if the person in the office provided information over the phone.

Call back and speak to the accountant directly about the phone call and explain your concerns and the importance of keeping your information private. Then, by fax or telephone, contact your lawyer and ask that a letter be sent to the accountant or a call be made on your behalf regarding your personal information.

Accountant *(Phone Number and Contact Sheet)*

Accountant

_____

(Name of Firm)

_____

_____

_____

(Address)

_____

(Phone Number)

_____

(Email)

_____

(Fax Number)

_____

(Contact Person)

PHONE LOG

REMARKS   **DATE**

1) _____   _____

2) _____   _____

3) _____   _____

4) _____   _____

5) _____   _____

6) _____   _____

7) _____   _____

8) _____   _____

9) _____   _____

10) _____   _____

YOU MAY USE THIS FORM TO NOTIFY YOUR ACCOUNTANT.

Date: _____

To: _____
                    (Name of Accountant)

_____
                    (Name of Firm)

Address: _____

City, State, Zip:_____

Dear _____:
                (Name of Person)

On _____, I spoke with _____ from your office.
            (Date)
This letter confirms the information provided to your office. I am requesting the following changes with

respect to my accounting records effective _____. Information pertaining to all my
                                                        (Date)
personal and/or business related matters will be kept confidential. I am also requesting the following

password of _____ be placed on my in-house records at your firm. No

information is to be provided to anyone without first providing you this password. If you receive a court

order from a judge asking for the release of my records, I ask that you contact me immediately at

_____ or my attorney _____ at
            (Phone Number)   *(Name of Attorney)*
_____.
        (Attorney's Phone Number)

In addition, please direct all billing inquiries to: _____

_____

Thank you in advance for your assistance.

Sincerely,

_____

You may be seeing a therapist or counselor. Maybe you are taking a medication such as an anti-depressant. While it is a widely used prescription, this information may be used against you in a divorce. Even with the privacy act in place, where health care providers are prohibited from releasing information, this information can still be released.

If you are in a custody battle, maybe your spouse is trying to get prescription or doctors' records for his lawyer. Maybe he knows the person who works at these places and knows that he can gather what he needs.

Perhaps bills will be thrown out and all of a sudden your credit is affected because they were unpaid or not submitted to the insurance company.

You could also be waiting for letters or appointment information via the mail and if you have moved, or are concerned you won't receive the information, it's best to fill out (Form E) and send it to the appropriate medical offices.

Once you have sent this form via registered mail, call to make sure that your efforts to secure your information is documented in your file.

In addition to the above information, make an appointment for medical checkups, yearly exams, or changes in your medication. Medical problems due to stress can suddenly appear when you least expect it.

Staple or clip a copy of all returned receipts to this page.

Medical *(Phone Number and Contact Sheet)*

_____   _____   _____
(Name of Company)   (Phone Number)   (Date)

_____   Follow Up Remarks: _____
(Spoke With)

_____

_____

_____   _____   _____
(Name of Company)   (Phone Number)   (Date)

_____   Follow Up Remarks: _____
(Spoke With)

_____

_____

_____   _____   _____
(Name of Company)   (Phone Number)   (Date)

_____   Follow Up Remarks: _____
(Spoke With)

_____

_____

_____   _____   _____
(Name of Company)   (Phone Number)   (Date)

_____   Follow Up Remarks: _____
(Spoke With)

_____

_____

_____   _____   _____
(Name of Company)   (Phone Number)   (Date)

_____   Follow Up Remarks: _____
(Spoke With)

_____

_____

YOU MAY USE THIS FORM TO NOTIFY ANY HEALTH CARE PROVIDERS, DOCTORS, THERAPISTS, PHARMACY, HEALTH INSURANCE PROVIDER AND/OR OTHERS.

Date: _____

To: _____

Address: _____

City, State, Zip:_____

RE: _____
              (Social Security Number)

Dear Doctor _____:
              (Name of Doctor)

On _____, I spoke with _____ from your office.
      (Date)

I am requesting that any medical information, files, notes, etc., remain confidential. At no time do you have authorization to release any information pertaining to myself or any member of my family without a certified court order which should first be sent to: _____ for
                                      (Name of Lawyer)

verification and their telephone number is _____.

In addition, please put the following password of _____ on my records. If you receive a call asking whether I am a patient or requesting information over the phone, unless you are first given the authorized password, no information is to be released. This includes address or telephone information you have on file. Finally, I am requesting that you post a restricted access alert on your computer system regarding this information. Please direct all communications, including billing inquiries to the following address: _____

_____

If you need to speak with me, I can be reached at _____

Additional comments: _____

_____

Thank you in advance for your assistance.

Sincerely,

_____

Ask Yourself the Following Questions

• Do you know where all your credit cards are?
• Do you know how many you have?
• Have you saved the envelope and the insert in which the credit card came?

Gather together all of your misplaced envelopes and credit cards, phone cards, cash station cards, and debit cards.

If the credit cards are in both of your names, see if you can get one just for you. Have your name removed from the joint credit card account. At the same time, place a password on the account. This will stop additional spending while your name is on the account. Try to do as much of this as you can while you are still living in the home.

When calling the card companies, place the call from your home number so that they know they are speaking with you. If you have asked for a new credit card, remember you will have to call from your home number to activate the card.

When the first bill arrives, change the address at the same time you make a payment, or change it on-line, but do not use your home computer.

For the credit card form (Form F) you will be adding two separate passwords. Why? Often someone is able to guess the first password, but it is unlikely they will they guess the second.

After you have sent in the form, call to make sure that two passwords are on the account. If not, ask to speak with a supervisor.

Staple or clip a copy of all returned receipts to this page.

Credit Cards *(Phone Number and Contact Sheet)*

Credit Cards

1) _____   _____   _____
       (Name of Company)   *(Card Number)*   *(Expiration Date)*

2) _____   _____   _____
       (Name of Company)   *(Card Number)*   *(Expiration Date)*

3) _____   _____   _____
       (Name of Company)   *(Card Number)*   *(Expiration Date)*

4) _____   _____   _____
       (Name of Company)   *(Card Number)*   *(Expiration Date)*

5) _____   _____   _____
       (Name of Company)   *(Card Number)*   *(Expiration Date)*

6) _____   _____   _____
       (Name of Company)   *(Card Number)*   *(Expiration Date)*

7) _____   _____   _____
       (Name of Company)   *(Card Number)*   *(Expiration Date)*

(Name of Company)   *(Phone Number)*   *(Date)*
(Spoke With)   Follow Up Remarks: _____

(Name of Company)   *(Phone Number)*   *(Date)*
(Spoke With)   Follow Up Remarks: _____

(Name of Company)   *(Phone Number)*   *(Date)*
(Spoke With)   Follow Up Remarks: _____

YOU MAY USE THIS FORM TO NOTIFY CREDIT CARD COMPANIES.

Date: _____

To: _____
       (Name of Company)
Address: _____   From: _____

City, State, Zip: _____   Address: _____

RE: _____   City, State, Zip: _____
       (Account Number)

_____
(Social Security Number)

TO WHOM IT MAY CONCERN:

On _____, I spoke with _____ from your office.
            (Date)
I am requesting the following changes be made to my account. They are as follows:

_____

_____

_____
(If you were the primary credit card holder and wish the other persons name to be removed, please include here. If you are making an address change, provide the new address etc.)

As an additional safety precaution, I am requesting that **two** passwords of _____

and _____ be placed on my account information in order to access my

records. The changes are to begin effectively on _____.

Should you wish to contact me I can be reached at _____ or _____.
                                                        (Day)   *(Evening)*
Thank you in advance for your assistance.

Sincerely,

_____

YOU MAY USE THIS FORM TO NOTIFY CREDIT CARD COMPANIES.

Date: _____

To: _____
(Name of Company)

Address: _____   From: _____

City, State, Zip: _____   Address: _____

RE: _____   City, State, Zip: _____
(Account Number)

_____
(Social Security Number)

TO WHOM IT MAY CONCERN:

On _____, I spoke with _____ from your office.
(Date)

I am requesting the following changes be made to my account. They are as follows:

_____

_____

_____

(If you were the primary credit card holder and wish the other persons name to be removed, please include here. If you are making an address change, provide the new address etc.)

As an additional safety precaution, I am requesting that **two** passwords of _____

and _____ be placed on my account information in order to access my

records. The changes are to begin effectively on _____.

Should you wish to contact me I can be reached at _____ or _____.
(Day)   *(Evening)*

Thank you in advance for your assistance.

Sincerely,

_____

YOU MAY USE THIS FORM TO NOTIFY CREDIT CARD COMPANIES.

Date: _____

To: _____
    (Name of Company)

Address: _____

From: _____

City, State, Zip: _____

Address: _____

RE: _____
    (Account Number)

City, State, Zip: _____

_____
(Social Security Number)

TO WHOM IT MAY CONCERN:

On _____, I spoke with _____ from your office.
    (Date)

I am requesting the following changes be made to my account. They are as follows:

_____

_____

_____

(If you were the primary credit card holder and wish the other persons name to be removed, please include here. If you are making an address change, provide the new address etc.)

As an additional safety precaution, I am requesting that **two** passwords of _____

and _____ be placed on my account information in order to access my

records. The changes are to begin effectively on _____.

Should you wish to contact me I can be reached at _____ or _____.
                                                         (Day)   *(Evening)*

Thank you in advance for your assistance.

Sincerely,

_____

Credit Cards

YOU MAY USE THIS FORM TO NOTIFY CREDIT CARD COMPANIES.

Date: _____

To: _____
                (Name of Company)

Address: _____

City, State, Zip: _____

RE: _____
             (Account Number)

_____
     (Social Security Number)

From: _____

Address: _____

City, State, Zip: _____

TO WHOM IT MAY CONCERN:

On _____, I spoke with _____ from your office.
        (Date)

I am requesting the following changes be made to my account. They are as follows:

_____

_____

_____

(If you were the primary credit card holder and wish the other persons name to be removed, please include here. If you are making an address change, provide the new address etc.)

As an additional safety precaution, I am requesting that **two** passwords of _____

and _____ be placed on my account information in order to access my

records. The changes are to begin effectively on _____.

Should you wish to contact me I can be reached at _____ or _____.
                                     (Day)   *(Evening)*

Thank you in advance for your assistance.

Sincerely,

_____

Credit Report Request

YOU MAY USE THIS FORM TO REQUEST YOUR CREDIT REPORT.

Date: _____

To: _____
                (Name of Credit Agency)

Address: _____

City, State, Zip:_____

TO WHOM IT MAY CONCERN:

According to my credit report, your data base records indicate credit information that is not correct.

My personal Information is as follows:

Name: _____ Social Security Number: _____

Date of Birth: _____ Length at present address: _____

Address: _____

_____

The following information is not correct: _____

_____

_____

This needs to be amended on my report because (explain why and provide the details) _____

_____

_____

In sending this letter, I am formally requesting that your agency contact the listed creditor and have them prove that this information is correct; otherwise delete this unfounded information from my credit report. For safety reasons, please do not provide access to my information unless you are given _____ as a password. I am requesting this be listed in your database, prior to releasing my credit information. With this letter, I hereby place you on notice, in accordance with applicable federal and state laws, that you make this letter a permanent part of my credit record with your agency.

Thank you for your assistance.

Sincerely,

_____

State by State

Alabama
P.O. Box 671
Montgomery, AL 36101
334.269.1515
www.alabar.org

Alaska
P.O. Box 100279
Anchorage, AK 99511
907.272.0352
www.alaskabar.org

Arizona
111 West Monroe, Suite 1800
Phoenix, AZ 85003
602.252.4804
www.azbar.org

Arkansas
400 W. Markham St.
Little Rock, AR 72201
501.375.4605
www.arkbar.com

California
1149 South Hill St.
Los Angeles, CA 90015
213.765.1000
www.calbar.org

Colorado
1900 Grant Street, Suite 950
Denver, CO 80203
303.860.1115
www.cobar.org

Connecticut
30 Bank Street
P.O. Box 350
New Britain, CT 06050-0350
860.223.4400
www.ctbar.org

Delaware
1201 Orange Street
Wilmington, DE 19801
302.658.5279
www.dsba.org

District of Columbia
1250 H St., N.W.
Washington, DC 20005
202.737.4700
www.dcbar.org

Florida
650 Appalachia Pkwy
Tallahassee, FL 32399-3200
850.561.5600
www.flabar.org

Georgia
800 The Hurt Bldg.
50 Hurt Plaza
Atlanta, GA 30303
404.527.8700
www.gabar.org

Hawaii
1132 Bishop, Suite 906
Honolulu, HI 96813
808.537.1868
www.hsba.org

Idaho
525 W. Jefferson St.
Boise, ID 83701
208.334.4500
www.state.id.us/isb

Illinois
424 S. Second St.
Springfield, IL 62701
217.525.1760
www.illinoisbar.org

Indiana
230 East Ohio St., 4th Floor
Indianapolis, IN 46204
317.639.5465
www.inbar.org

Iowa
521 E. Locust St., Suite 300
Des Moines, IA 50309-1939
515.243.3179
www.iowabar.org

Kansas
1200 SW Harrison
Topeka, KS 66601-1037
785.234.5696
www.ksbar.org

Kentucky
514 W. Main St.
Frankfort, KY 40601
502.564.3795
www.kybar.org

Louisiana
601 St. Charles Ave.
New Orleans, LA 70130
504.566.1600
www.lsba.org

Maine
124 State St.
P.O Box 788
Augusta, ME 04332
207.622.7523
www.mainebar.org

Maryland
520 West Sayette St.
Baltimore, MD 21201
410.685.7878
www.msba.org

American Bar Association Offices

State by State (continued)

Massachusetts
20 West St.
Boston, MA 02111
617.542.3602
www.massbar.org

Michigan
306 Townsend St.
Lansing, MI 48933
517.372.9030
www.michbar.org

Minnesota
600 Nicolette Mall, Suite 380
Minneapolis, MN 55402
612.333.1183
www.mnbar.org

Mississippi
P.O. Box 2168
Jackson, MS 39225-2168
601.948.4471
www.msbar.org

Missouri
326 Monroe St.
Jefferson City, MO 65101
573.635.4128
www.mobar.org

Montana
P.O. Box 577
Helena, MT 59624
406.442.7660
www.montanabar.org

Nebraska
635 South 14th St.
Lincoln, NE 68501
402.475.7091
www.nebar.com

Nevada
600 East Charleston
Las Vegas, NV 89104
775.329.4100
www.nvbar.org

New Hampshire
112 Pleasant St.
Concord, NH 03301
603.224.6942
www.nhbar.org

New Jersey
1 constitution Square
New Brunswick, NJ 08901
732.249.5000
www.njsba.com

New Mexico
P.O Box 25883
Albuquerque, NM 87125
505.797.6000
www.nmbar.org

New York
One Elk St.
Albany, NY 12207
518.463.3200
www.nysba.org

North Carolina
P.O. Box 25908
Raleigh, NC 27611
919.828.4620
www.ncbar.com

North Dakota
515½ East Broadway
Bismarck, ND 58502-0530
800.472.2685
www.sband.org

Ohio
1700 Lake Shore Dr.
P.O. Box 16562
Columbus, OH 43216-16562
614.487.2050
www.ohiobar.org

Oklahoma
P.O. Box 53036
Oklahoma City, OK 73152
405.524.2365
www.okbar.org

Oregon
P.O. Box 1689
Lake Oswego, OR 97035
503.620.0222
www.osbar.org

Pennsylvania
100 South St.
P.O. Box 186
Harrisburg, PA 17108
717.238.6715
www.pabar.org

Rhode Island
115 Cedar St.
Providence, RI 02903
401.421.5740
www.ribar.com

South Carolina
P.O. Box 608
Columbia, SC 29292.0608
803.799.6653
www.scbar.org

State by State (continued)

South Dakota
222 East Capitol Ave.
Pierre, SD 57501
605.224.7554
www.sdbar.org

Tennessee
3622 West End Ave.
Nashville, TN 37205
615.383.7421
www.tba.org

Texas
P.O. Box 12487
Austin, TX 78711
512.463.1463
www.texasbar.com

Utah
654 S. 200 East St.
Salt Lake City, UT 84111
801.531.9110
www.utahbar.org

Vermont
P.O. Box 100
Montpelier, VT 05601
802.223.2020
www.vtbar.org

Virginia
707 East Main St., Suite 1500
Richmond, VA 23219-2803
804.775.0500
www.vsb.org

Washington
2104 4th Ave. 4th Floor
Seattle, WA 90121
206.727.8200
www.wsba.org

West Virginia
2006 Kanawha Blvd East
Charleston, WV 25311
304.558.2456
www.wvbar.org

Wisconsin
P.O. Box 7158
Madison, WI 53707-7158
608.257.3838
www.wisbar.org

Wyoming
P.O. Box 109
Cheyenne, WY 82003
307.632.9061
www.wyomingbar.org

84

This guide provides resources to help you in many areas of your life.

- AGENCY FOR HEALTH CARE POLICY AND RESEARCH CLEARINGHOUSE

- ALCOHOLICS ANONYMOUS

- AMERICANS WITH DISABILITIES INFORMATION LINE

- AUTO

- BREAST HEALTH ACCESS FOR WOMEN WITH DISABILITIES

- MY BUDGET PLANNER

- CENTER FOR DISEASE CONTROL-National Immunization Program

- CENTER FOR DISEASE CONTROL-National AIDS Hotline

- CENTER FOR DISEASE CONTROL-National AIDS Clearinghouse

- CENTERS FOR INDEPENDENT LIVING

- CHILD SUPPORT ENFORCEMENT ABROAD

- DEPARTMENT OF MOTOR VEHICLES

- DIVORCE SOURCE

- FEDERAL CITIZEN INFORMATION CENTER

- FEDERAL GOVERNMENT INFORMATION LINE

- FINANCIAL

- FOOD STAMP PROGRAM

- GOVERNMENT RESOURCES

- HEALTHFINDER

- HEALTH INSURANCE

- INSURANCE QUOTES

- JOB OPPORTUNITIES

- LEGAL
  - State-by-State Legal Resources for Domestic Violence Victims
  - Listing of State-by-State Child Support Enforcement
  - Dedicated in getting unpaid court ordered child support
  - Resources for unpaid child support in Canada
  - Helps parents get child support

- NATIONAL CLEARINGHOUSE FOR ALCOHOL AND DRUG INFORMATION

- NATIONAL COALITION AGAINST DOMESTIC VIOLENCE

- NATIONAL DAYCARE REFERRAL AGENCY

- NATIONAL DRUG INFORMATION, TREATMENT AND REFERRAL LINE

- NATIONAL HEADACHE FOUNDATION

- NATIONAL ORGANIZATION FOR VICTIM ASSISTANCE

- NATIONAL RUNAWAY SWITCHBOARD

- NATIONAL WOMEN'S HEALTH INFORMATION CENTER

- OFFICE OF CITIZENSHIP, APPEALS AND LEGAL ASSISTANCE

- OFFICE OF PERSONNEL MANAGEMENT

- SALVATION ARMY

- SOCIAL SECURITY INFORMATION

AGENCY FOR HEALTH CARE POLICY AND RESEARCH CLEARINGHOUSE

A free guide titled: *Prescription Medicines and You*, is available.
Phone: 800.358.9295
Website: www.ahcpr.gov/consumer/ncpiebro.htm

ALCOHOLICS ANONYMOUS

A network of mutual support groups for recovering alcoholics. See your local telephone White Pages for local groups.
Phone: 212.870.3400

AMERICANS WITH DISABILITIES INFORMATION LINE

U.S. Department of Justice
Phone: 800.514.0301 TDD: 800.514.0383
Website: www.usdoj.gov/crt/ada/infoline.htm

AUTO

Contains free advice about car repairs, how to find a reputable mechanic etc.
Website: www.my-auto-mechanic.com

BREAST HEALTH ACCESS FOR WOMEN WITH DISABILITIES

Offers breast health information, screenings and early Breast Cancer detection.
Phone: 510.204.4866 TDD: 510.204.4574
Website: www.bhawd.org/sitefiles/index2.html

MY BUDGET PLANNER

Assists you with budgeting, planning, and spending.
Website: www.mybudgetplanner.com

CENTER FOR DISEASE CONTROL
National Immunization Program

Phone: 800.232.0233 Website: www.cdc.gov
Spanish Immunization hotline: 800.232.0233
English Immunization hotline: 800.CDC.SHOT

Center on Disease Control-National Aids Hotline

Phone: 800.342.AIDS (English)
800.344.7432 (Spanish) TDD: 800.243.7889

Center on Disease Control-National AIDS Clearinghouse

Phone: 800.458.5231 TDD: 800.243.7012
Website: www.cdcnpin.org

CENTERS FOR INDEPENDENT LIVING

An information site for people with disabilities.
Website: www.ilusa.com

CHILD SUPPORT ENFORCEMENT ABROAD

This site offers step-by-step guidance, general information, and reference resources from the U.S. State Department. This is a good site for parents and lawyers trying to enforce child support when the person required to make payments has left the country.
Website: www.travel.state.gov/family/child-support.html

DEPARTMENT OF MOTOR VEHICLES

Offices are located in every state and usually in every county seat municipality. Each state has different regulations about the information they will release to an individual. The police working on your case will probably be able to access the records more easily, once criminal charges have been filed.

DIVORCE SOURCE

This interactive site includes discussion forums pertaining to divorce issues, including custody and visitation, parental abduction, and domestic violence. This site also features helpful resource services and books that might be of assistance.
Website: www.divorcesource.com

Resource Guide (continued)

FEDERAL CITIZEN INFORMATION CENTER
Phone: 800.FED.INFO
TDD: 800.326.2996 (hearing-impaired)

FEDERAL GOVERNMENT INFORMATION LINE
You can gain information on how to request information under the Federal Freedom of Information Act.
Phone: 800.688.9889

FINANCIAL
An on-line financial resource for single moms.
Website: www.making-ends-meet.org

FOOD STAMP PROGRAM
Provides information on how to apply for food stamps. Also directs people who would like to help friends or relatives acquire food stamps.
Website: www.fns.usda.gov/fsp/

GOVERNMENT RESOURCES
This government guide, available on-line, offers welfare and low income assistance, and child support information that includes enforcement. This site also includes food stamps, health insurance, housing and heating assistance, legal aid, senior services, and information on domestic violence.
Website: governmentguide.com/benefits/welfare

HEALTH FINDER
A website service created by the U.S. Department of Health and Human Services offering information on health care, health information links and an A to Z online library.
Website: http://www.healthfinder.gov/

HEALTH INSURANCE
Low cost health insurance for children.
Website: www.insurekidsnow.gov

INSURANCE QUOTES
Quotesmith maintains a database of approximately 350 health insurance companies across the country. This service allows you to get instant quotes for life, medical, auto, and dental insurance as well as Medicare supplements if you are 65 or over. If you do not have a computer, you can call them at 800.556.9393, 7 am to 10 pm Monday through Friday, and 8 am to 5 pm Saturday (Central time).
Website: www.quotesmith.com

JOB OPPORTUNITIES
Job opportunities for low income people
Website: www.govbenefits.gov/index.jsp

Assists you with resumes, computer skills, employment services, and a GED diploma
Website: www.transform-me.org

LEGAL
State-by-State legal resources for domestic violence victims
Website: www.womenslaw.org

Listing of State-by-State Child Support Enforcement
Website: www.divorcenet.com

Dedicated in getting unpaid court ordered child support
Website: www.wantedposters.com

Resources for unpaid child support in Canada
Website: www.Fadcanada.org

Helps parents get child support
Website: www.nationalchildsupport.com

NATIONAL CLEARINGHOUSE FOR ALCOHOL AND DRUG INFORMATION

Focuses on preventive and health-related info.
Phone: 800.729.6686
Website: www.health.org

NATIONAL COALITION AGAINST DOMESTIC VIOLENCE

Provides information on battered women's shelters in your area, 24 hours a day 7 days a week.
National Hotline: 800.799.7233
TDD: 800.787.3224

NATIONAL DAYCARE REFERRAL AGENCY

For assistance in finding quality daycare and referral.
Phone: 800.424.2246

THE NATIONAL DRUG INFORMATION, TREATMENT AND REFERRAL LINE

Free and confidential. The hours are 9 am-3 am (Monday-Friday) and 12 noon-3 am (Saturday-Sunday).
Phone: 800.662.HELP or
800.66.AYUDA (Spanish)
Website: www.drughelp.org

NATIONAL HEADACHE FOUNDATION

A good resource with information on the latest in headache causes and treatments. Includes self management tips to minimize the impact of headaches in your life.
Phone: 888.NHF.5552
Website: www.headaches.org

NATIONAL ORGANIZATION FOR VICTIM ASSISTANCE

Publishes a newsletter, NOVA, and maintains a national directory of services for victims of all types.
Phone: 800.879.6682
Website: www.try-nova.org

NATIONAL RUNAWAY SWITCHBOARD

Phone: 800.621.4000 TDD: 800.621.0394
Website: www.nrscrisline.org

NATIONAL WOMEN'S HEALTH INFORMATION CENTER

Provides a free, reliable health information to women everywhere.
Phone: 800.994.9662
Website: www.4women.gov

Women with Disabilities web page
Phone: 800.994.9662 TDD: 888.220.5446
Website: www.4woman.gov/wwd

OFFICE OF CITIZENSHIP, APPEALS AND LEGAL ASSISTANCE

1425 K Street, NW Rm. 300
Washington, D.C. 20522
Phone: 202.326.6168

OFFICE OF PERSONNEL MANAGEMENT

Can locate retired or active civil service or military personnel.
1900 E. Street, NW, Washington, D.C. 20415
Phone: 202.606.2424

SALVATION ARMY

They provide emergency lodging, food, and shelter across America. See your Yellow Pages for the nearest location. Or you can write: Post Office Box 269, Alexandria, VA 22313

SOCIAL SECURITY INFORMATION

Phone: 800.772.1213 TDD: 800.325.0778
Website: www.ssa.gov

College Resources

Today the Internet makes researching colleges a simple task. When families split, often the money that could have been used for your child's college education goes directly to the divorce lawyers or the time needed to properly research options just is not available. If you don't have access to a computer, go to your local library and use its Internet access, or look for books on college applications, how to write application essays, or information on various schools and scholarships.

To apply for federal financial aid, and to apply for many student aid programs, students must complete a Free Application for Federal Student Aid (FAFSA). Electronic versions of the FAFSA make applying for financial aid faster and easier than ever.

If you have any questions, or require additional information on student financial assistance, you may contact your high school guidance counselor, the financial aid officer at the post-secondary institution you plan to attend, or the Federal Student Aid Information Center, open Monday through Friday, from 8 am to 8 pm (Eastern Time).

COLLEGE BOARD CONTACT INFORMATION

This site has a wealth of information about the College Board's resources.
Website: www.collegeboard.org

COLLEGE CREDIT EDUCATION LOAN PROGRAM

Students interested in applying for College Credit Education Loans should call 800.832.5626 or contact their aid administrators. For additional information about College Credit, contact: Jennifer Jenkins, Manager; College Credit Education Loan Program; The College Board: 11911 Freedom Drive, Suite 400, Reston, VA 20190
Phone: 800.626.9795 or 703.707.8999
Fax: 708.707.5599
E-mail: College Credit@collegeboard.org

CSS/FINANCIAL AID PROFILE

Students with questions or comments about PRO-FILE should call CSS at 305.829.9793 from 8 am to 10 pm, Eastern Time, Sunday through Friday, from September 15 to April 1. After April 1, service hours are 8 am to 6 pm. Eastern Time, Monday through Friday, and are subject to change.

Financial aid administrators or high school counselors with questions and comments about PROFILE should contact one of the CSS Regional Offices. Also call to order additional copies of the PROFILE Registration Guide or the PROFILE Basic Application.
Phone: 800.239.5888. TDD: 800.915.9990
E-mail: help@cssprofile.org

FEDERAL STUDENT AID INFORMATION CENTER

Phone: 800.4.FED.AID (1.800.433.3243)

SCHOLARSHIPS AND SEARCH SERVICES

Financial aid offers from colleges are not the only source of assistance available to students. Millions of dollars are given away each year to deserving students by private organizations. Finding these scholarships and applying for them can be a frustrating, but rewarding process.

The best place to start looking for scholarships is in your high school guidance office. Once you have a handle on what is available locally, it is time to use the free scholarship search services available on the Internet.
Website: www.theoldschool.org/scholars.asp

College Resources (continued)

SERVICE ACADEMIES
for information write:

UNITED STATES AIR FORCE ACADEMY
Colorado Springs, CO 80840

UNITED STATES COAST GUARD ACADEMY
New London, CT 06320

UNITED STATES MERCHANT MARINE ACADEMY
Kings Point, NY 10204

UNITED STATES MILITARY ACADEMY
West Point, NY 10996

UNITED STATES NAVAL ACADEMY
Annapolis, MD 21402

SCHOLARSHIPS AND FINANCIAL AID SOURCES ON THE INTERNET
This site contains information regarding general scholarships, universities, and colleges.
Website: www.uscsu.sc.edu/student_affairs/scholar.htm

Abusive Relationships

A turning point in my life came one wintry Chicago evening, when I entered my parent's home. It would be for the last time, and the day my life changed forever.

My mother, after 28 years of abuse, had divorced my father who was a Chicago police detective. After the divorce, the stalking and harassing phone calls continued. Like so many abusers, my father was cunning, clever, and manipulative. I was always afraid that he would do something to hurt her. My father always looked at my mother as his personal property. I had asked the lawyer, who represented my mother, to have my mother sign a quitclaim deed, which she did. If the attorney had explained it properly to her, she would have understood that no further signature was necessary.

That morning, my father asked her to come to their marital residence to sign papers for the sale of the home. This was just a ploy to get her to return to the house alone. My mother thought the abuse was behind her. She, like many other women, did not believe that he would follow through with his threats. He was not going to allow her life to continue, unless he could continue to control her. When he lost all control, he killed her and then himself. That day I swore that I would do everything in my power to prevent this from happening to another woman. It was not until I began assisting others that I realized how important it is to have a safety plan.

When emotions run high it is often difficult to know what direction to take. Abuse is often not just about slapping, hitting, or punching. It is about the person who tells us one minute that they love us and that we can never do anything right the next. Signs can include extreme jealousy and possessiveness. The abuser might attempt to isolate their victim by using threats and intimidation.

Emotional abuse can be just as painful as physical abuse. You cannot see the scars on the outside like with physical abuse, but they live deep inside you.

CAROL'S STORY
How Do You Begin to Move On?

Carol is a woman who married when she was 18. Now after two children and 30 years of marriage she has had enough. She is with a man who abuses her almost daily. "Mostly he's verbally abusive telling me I'm stupid, that he doesn't know why he stays with me, or I'm not as pretty as I use to be. He does not hit me anymore. But when he ignores me, as if I am invisible, or gives me those cold stares of his, it feels the same as when he used to slap me."

She works a full time job so she can have her own money, and has saved enough to move out, find a lawyer, and get on with her life. When I asked her what her husband's yearly salary was, she had no clue. He bought a business last year and he is very secretive about the company and what was required financially to purchase it. "Every year at tax time he places the tax returns in front of me, puts a pen in my hand and points to where I am supposed to sign. I am not allowed to look it over or ask any questions. I wasn't raised this way, I never saw my parents fight; my home was very loving and supportive."

Carol knows where the household financial records are kept and she will make copies of whatever is there. Her husband uses their home computer to make banking transactions and credit card payments. With their home computer she is able to do a number of things. First, she located the credit card numbers. She went on-line using his credit card number, his social security number, and his mother's maiden name. When her attempts at access failed she used the "I forgot my password" prompt. The computer asked the question: What city are you from? She knew the answer and entered it on the screen. Success!

Carol was able to download every transaction from the previous two years and print it out. In this case, the banking information was a bit easier because he had a sheet with account numbers and passwords hidden in a file marked cemetery plots. Once Carol was on-line, she was able to retrieve and print almost three full years of bank statements.

Gathering this financial information will save her money when she hires legal representation. Carol has no idea what she will need to live on, but she is creating a budget and a safety plan that will be easier to follow.

BARBARA'S STORY
Money Isn't Everything

I was in my last year of college when I met and married a man from a wealthy family with a country club life style. I wanted out after three weeks. He was badmouthing my friends and family and making it impossible for me to maintain contact with anyone but his friends. In public, we were the perfect couple. However, inside I was dying.

Every step I took was under his watchful eye. Looking back now, I know he had many affairs. His own mother had never said a word to his father about the many women he had in his life and so, to my husband, that was an acceptable way of life. I was on a tight household budget and only allowed to buy the basics. He, however, spent lavishly on boats, trips, and women. If we went on vacation, it was only so I could be servant, maid, and babysitter to his friends. The household income was well over $200,000.

When I requested some money for blinds and repairs, he blew up. I realized after 11 years of marriage that I was not living for me or us, just him. Therefore, I learned to stop asking for things. When I did, he would tell me I was worthless and pathetic. He was controlling everything from what I watched on television to not being allowed to attend church.

I had had enough, and yet, I still wanted to make the marriage work. When I suggested we both go to counseling he refused, saying the "marriage was perfectly fine." So I thought, to heck with him I will go myself. The counselor told me that I was a victim of severe emotional abuse. I finally heard the words. It took a complete stranger, but I finally listened. After six months of therapy, I asked for a marital separation. A couple weeks later, he removed all financial documents from the house. I later learned he was stashing large amounts of money away.

I filed for divorce. When he got a new girlfriend, he moved out. His flaunting of the relationship did not bother me as much as his abusive behavior towards me. After three years, I am still in court. We go to trial in a few weeks. During the past three years, he went against numerous court orders to pay temporary support and the household bills.

He has liquidated large sums of money and assets, which I discovered only after hiring a private and reputable investigator. It is only with support of family, friends, and church that I am able to go on with my life. I would pray for him but his God is the almighty dollar.

ELIZABETH'S STORY
Marriage The Second Time Around

My first marriage ended with my walking away with the clothes on my back, my children, and my car. I literally had to start again. Within a year, with the help of family and friends, I was back on my feet.

I swore that I would never have another relationship. That is until I met Patrick at a friend's wedding. Things were different. He had a great job, he was warm and kind to me, and most of all he treated my children from a previous marriage as if they were his own. We were truly happy. Due to our financial situation, I was able to be a stay-at-home mom. After about two years of marriage, Patrick was laid off from his job. I was happy to go back to work to help with the household expenses until he got back on his feet. We both worked different shifts and one of us was home with the children at all times. Things began to happen that I wish I had paid attention to, but I did not. That is until one day, my 13-year-old daughter's principal called to inform me that her stepfather had been molesting her.

Horror, disbelief, every emotion imaginable flooded in. My world crumbled before me and things were never the same after that. It has been two years since the divorce and my daughter and I are still dealing with this everyday. The very foundation of my being has been shattered like tiny pieces of glass on the floor. I lost myself as a mother, wife, and person.

I love my kids with every fiber of my being and that is what keeps me going. My hope is that with continued counseling; maybe someday, I can put the pieces of my family back together again.

THE CHILDREN

My mother often had to come in and break up fist fights between my brother and me. Because I was older and bigger, I would pretend to be my father and my brother had no choice but to take the role of my mother. I would point to my brother and repeat my father's words, "Little children should be seen and not heard." Sometimes I would pretend to be my father and push my brother around and say, "You better do what I say or else." Then I would punch my finger into his chest and, imitating my father, shout, "Do you understand me?"

Parents must consider what kind of example they are setting for their children. Adults often decide that they are doing what is best for the children by keeping the family together. Children, who grow up in violent homes, usually wind up using violence or control as their method of dealing with problem solving and coping in their adult lives. To grow up, as I did, in a family where your father repeatedly beats your mother, is indeed a devastating experience with a lifetime of damaging consequences. The scars children develop inside can be just as damaging as those that are physically inflicted.

YOU CAN BE FREE OF AN ABUSIVE RELATIONSHIP

Every situation is different; like our own individual fingerprints, no two relationships are alike. Victims do have two things in common: a need to be safe and a need to get out.

This guide provides you with the tools you need on your journey. Obtaining a court order of protection can be your first step toward showing the abuser that you will not allow the abusive behavior to continue and that you are serious. Many women leave because they realize that in order to begin a new life; they must first remove themselves from danger.

JUDY'S STORY
"I Didn't Deserve To Be Abused."

When Judy and her husband married, they were very happy, like all newlyweds. Her husband was a hard working man and they looked forward to building a new life together. "I remember coming home to share the news that we were going to have a baby." My husband was angry and upset. "How could you let this happen, you little bitch?" He told me to abort the baby. Then with his boot he began kicking me in my side and stomach. I screamed for someone to help me, but no one heard. When he turned around and walked out the door, I dialed 911 for police assistance.

When the police arrived, they called an ambulance to take me to the hospital. I was so scared and numb. He had never acted like this before.

That night he never came home. The police said I could get a temporary restraining order from the court. When I awoke the following morning, my face and body were bruised and swollen, but thank goodness, the baby was going to be okay.

I got dressed and headed for the court building, filed the paperwork, signed a complaint, went before the judge, and received my temporary restraining order. The Judge told me that if my husband showed up at the apartment, I should call the police immediately and they would arrest him for battery.

When I got home, I called the landlord and had the locks changed. The following night he broke into the apartment from the back door. When I heard the sound of breaking glass hit the kitchen floor, I dialed 911. Within minutes, the police arrived and took him to jail.

When my apartment lease was up I arranged to move out immediately, just before the baby was born. On the final court date, six months after the attack, the Judge issued me a two-year order of protection and my husband was given one year's probation.

Abusive Relationships *(continued)*

I knew that I had to take steps to get a divorce. With no money to speak of, I contacted several legal aid services provided to me in court. I made an appointment and in about four weeks, I began the legal paperwork for divorce. After my baby was born, we went to live with my sister. One night as we were watching television, a brick came through the front window. Then we heard someone at the front door. My sister immediately called the police. I grabbed the baby and headed out the back to escape. We heard my husband's voice from behind; he was screaming and yelling, "I'm going to kill you. I'm going to kill both of you!" I handed the baby to my sister who was running in front of me. Then suddenly, he grabbed my shirt from behind, and began to drag me backwards. He pinned me to the ground. I struggled, but he was too strong and drunk. He was punching me. Then the police grasped him from behind. It took three officers to handcuff him. I knew my daughter and I were not safe; we had to go far away so that he could never hurt us again.

I gathered anything and everything of value and took it to a pawn shop in town. Once again, we returned to court. This time the judge revoked my husband's bond pending a hearing and a criminal court trial. He had also violated probation and the court order of protection that stated he was to have no contact with me or any members of my family.

When I returned home from court, I immediately began packing. I told my sister that someday I would return, but for now I was leaving town. With a suitcase in one arm and my daughter in the other, we headed for the airport. I had a childhood friend who lived in New York. Thank God we kept in touch. When I called her from the airport, she didn't ask a million questions. All she said was that she would meet us at the airport and help in anyway she could.

Now, four years have passed. In the spring I will be graduating from nursing school, with honors. I thank God everyday that my daughter and I are safe and I can't wait for the day when I will be able to call my social worker to have us taken off public assistance. Through counseling and some wonderful friends, I got my life back.

LEAVING ABUSIVE RELATIONSHIPS

It is important to allow yourself enough time when preparing to leave an abusive relationship, especially if you are married and have children. It can be very difficult, but it can be done.

It is also a good idea once you begin to create your plan, not to make phone calls from your home. When you need to make calls go to a pay phone, or use the phone at your friends, relatives, or place of employment. Most importantly, remember not to use your home computer.

Begin by drafting a "plan of action" for yourself. Start gathering copies of important papers like:
* Birth certificates for you and the children; get certified copies
* Social security cards
* Marriage certificate
* Insurance policies
* Make a record of all bank account numbers, 401K plan and credit union accts. (including any in your children's names); make copies
* Make copies of your income tax returns for the past three years
* Make copies of all titles or property information
* Try to get a couple of your spouse's pay stubs; make copies
* Make copies of any stocks, savings bonds, etc.
* Contact your doctor and dentist to get copies of all medical records, which you can either pick up in person or have mailed to a trusted relative or friend for safekeeping
* Children's school records; make copies
* Passports for you and the children
* Prescriptions for any medications that you and the children take (if possible stock up)
* Spare keys to the house, garage, car, safety deposit box, etc.
* If you wear prescription glasses or a hearing aid device, get an extra set made and keep them with your important documents
* Title to the car
* Contact the credit bureau and request a copy of your credit report; and remember to send a letter

(provided in the workbook) that will restrict access unless a password is provided
* Use the forms in this workbook to place passwords on utilities, bills, etc.
* Try to save money and open a bank account in your name
* Just before you are ready to leave, go to your bank, and withdraw what you can (this should be done on the day you are preparing to leave, because as money is withdrawn it will be reflected on the account balance either on that day or on the following day.) You do not want to take chances, especially if your partner must suddenly use an ATM card or make a withdrawal and discover the account balance has changed
* Use whatever cash advance you have available to open an individual interest bearing account
* If possible, take your home computer with you on the day you leave
* If you are unable to take the computer, remove all data, addresses; take the disks; use the internet guide we provided to assist you in deleting passwords and other information
* If you run a home based business and use a computer, change all your passwords, change your screen name, and change your internet service provider. Do not insert personal information into any on-line directories or data bases.
* Secure a private post office box. Either have someone you trust do this in his name, on your behalf (perhaps someone that your partner would not suspect or know) or go to a private company like "mail boxes etc." rather than a post office. Whenever possible, use this as your address. Use words such as suite or apartment number instead of the term post office box.
* Make address changes for your bills, bank accounts, etc., by using the forms provided. Try to avoid filling out a change of address at your original shared postal service.
* Get an unpublished/unlisted telephone number
* When preparing to move, ask someone you trust to rent a place, in his name, on your behalf.

• When hiring a moving company, use a small company. On the other hand, if you need to use a large company, have them move your items to a storage unit that has been secured in another person's name, then contact a small local moving company to move them for you.

If you have received an order of protection from the courts and you are preparing to move, contact your local police department, explain that you have a court order, and you are requesting they send an officer to your home while you are moving. If you do not have an order of protection, then now is a good time to get one.

HOW DOES A DOMESTIC VIOLENCE ORDER OFFER PROTECTION?

An order of protection is a court order that provides protection for victims of domestic abuse. You can obtain an order of protection on an emergency basis when there is a likelihood of harm or injury by the abuser. Typically, an emergency order of protection is obtained after an incident has occurred and a police report has been made. The incident allows you to petition the courts with the assistance of a state's attorney or county prosecutor, who works on your behalf without charge, for an emergency order of protection or temporary restraining order (it varies in each state).

The judge hears your case without the presence of the abuser. Then the judge makes a decision regarding the facts of your case, at which time the judge may grant a temporary emergency order of protection for a maximum of 21 days.

The abuser is then served by a sheriff or police officer a copy of the order prohibiting contact with you for a 21-day period. A court date is set for your abuser to appear before the judge. On the scheduled date, you and your abuser return to the court. You are represented by the state and your abuser is represented by either a private attorney or a public defender.

Then the judge, based on the information provided, decides to set a hearing date. Your order of protection will usually be continued until the outcome of the case.

Once you have the order:
• Report all incidents to the police immediately.
• If there is further abuse, contact the county prosecutor's office or state's attorney to update them.
• If you receive medical treatment for any injuries sustained, make sure you get a copy of your medical treatment report.
• Do not initiate any contact with the abuser.
• Always keep a copy of your order with you at all times. Make extra copies for your car, employer, etc.

For support, shelter, or additional information on what is available to you, we suggest you contact:
• Your local State's Attorney or Prosecutor's Office
• The Attorney General's Office
• Your local battered women's shelter and/or counseling center
• The local Bar Association

Telephone numbers for the above are listed in your local phone book. You can go to your local library for information on the laws and resources available in your state.

WHO IS PROTECTED UNDER THE ORDER OF PROTECTION?

- Spouse
- Former Spouse
- Parents
- Children
- Stepchildren
- Persons (current or past) in dating or engagement relationship

- Persons related by blood or marriage
- Persons sharing or formally sharing a common dwelling
- Persons who have a child in common
- Persons sharing a blood relationship

WHAT IS A CIVIL ORDER OF PROTECTION?

The procedure for a Civil Order of Protection varies from state to state. Any local or state women's organizations, lawyer, or State's Attorney will be happy to explain the procedures in your area. When you petition for a Civil Order of Protection, usually no criminal charges have been filed against the alleged abuser. Many seek this type of order when they file for divorce. It is important to obtain pictures for evidence and witnesses for your case. The order is effective for the same length of time as a Criminal Order of Protection and it is issued by a judge.

Once you have filed for an Order of Protection, restraining order, or an order prohibiting the alleged abuser from having any contact with you and it has been signed by a judge, it's a good idea to use the accompanying form (Form H) as an extra safety precaution.

Often when you are issued an Order of Protection the person who has been abusing you may not have been served with the paperwork by the police or sheriff. After you make four copies of your protection order, fill out the provided "police" form (Form H) as best you can. Notice your order does not have a picture or description for the police to refer to should the abuser try to make contact with you, so we have included an area for this on the following "police" form.

Take a copy of your Order of Protection and this completed form to the police station where you live and give it to the law enforcement person at the desk.

Explain that you are giving them a copy of the order along with the form so they can be aware of the situation and be prepared to respond if necessary. Ask for the business card of the officer to whom you gave the order/form, and request extra patrols in your area.

Place extra copies of your Order of Protection inside this book.

YOU MAY USE THIS FORM TO NOTIFY THE POLICE OR STATES ATTORNEY.

Date: _____

To: _____
       (Police District)

Address: _____

City, State, Zip:_____

RE: Court Issued Order of Protection
(Restraining Order, Temporary Restraining Order)

Attach a
Recent Photo

_____
(Look at the first page of your order and place the number you were issued on the line above)

TO WHOM IT MAY CONCERN:

I have attached a recent photo of _____and a copy of my court order of

protection. The document was issued on _____ and expires on _____.

The description of the person listed on the order is as follows:

_____ _____ _____ _____ _____
(Height)   *(Weight)*   *(Hair Color)*   *(Facial Hair)*   *(Other)*

The vehicle he/she drives is:

_____ _____ _____ _____ _____
(Make)   *(Model)*   *(Year)*   *(Color)*   *(License Plate)*

I am asking that you keep an extra watch on my home. The address is _____

_____

And my vehicle is:

_____ _____ _____ _____ _____
(Make)   *(Model)*   *(Year)*   *(Color)*   *(License Plate)*

I am providing this to you as an additional safety precaution as I am concerned for everyone listed on

the order.

I thank you in advance for your cooperation during this difficult time.

Sincerely,

_____

If your children attend daycare, school, after-school programs, sports activities, etc., and you have an order from the judge that prohibits your spouse or the children's father/mother from seeing, taking, or picking up the children, you will need to use the following form (FORM I). You need to give this, along with a copy of your court order, to the people in charge of the facility that your child attends during the day.

Explain to each person that under no circumstances should the person listed in the order be allowed to drive by, stop, or call. If that happens they are to contact the police first and then you.

Make sure that you are able to pass out pictures of the alleged offender to the teachers, daycare workers, or activities persons.

If you have a lawyer you should also notify him of the names, addresses, and places to which this information was provided.

While this order is in effect, under no circumstances, is anyone allowed to accept, take, or give messages or gifts to your children. If such an attempt is made, contact the police immediately to file a report. Instruct the childcare providers to do the same.

Children *(Phone Number and Contact Sheet)*

_____   _____   _____
(Name of School)   *(Address)*   *(Phone Number)*

_____   *Given copy on:* _____   *Remarks:* _____
(Contact Person)

_____

_____

_____

_____   _____   _____
(Name of School)   *(Address)*   *(Phone Number)*

_____   *Given copy on:* _____   *Remarks:* _____
(Contact Person)

_____

_____

_____

_____   _____   _____
(Name of School)   *(Address)*   *(Phone Number)*

_____   *Given copy on:* _____   *Remarks:* _____
(Contact Person)

_____

_____

_____

_____   _____   _____
(Name of School)   *(Address)*   *(Phone Number)*

_____   *Given copy on:* _____   *Remarks:* _____
(Contact Person)

_____

_____

_____

_____   _____   _____
(Name of School)   *(Address)*   *(Phone Number)*

_____   *Given copy on:* _____   *Remarks:* _____
(Contact Person)

_____

_____

YOU MAY USE THIS FORM TO NOTIFY THE SCHOOL YOUR CHILDREN ATTEND, DAYCARE OR CHILDCARE PROVIDER, TUTORS OR OTHER AFTER SCHOOL PROGRAMS.

Date: _____

ATTN: _____

Name of School/Daycare Facility/After School Program:

_____

Address: _____

City, State, Zip: _____

RE: _____
        (list children's names and ages here)

_____

_____

```
┌─────────────────────┐
│                     │
│                     │
│     Attach a        │
│   Recent Photo      │
│                     │
│                     │
└─────────────────────┘
```

Dear _____:

Attached is a recent photo of _____. Attached also is a court

order of protection issued on _____ which expires on _____.

This letter is to alert you and your staff that _____ may be attempting to see,

speak with, or pick-up the children which the court order prohibits. Should this happen, you are to call

the police immediately and then notify _____ _____
                                                 (Name of Person)   *(Phone Number)*

or _____. As an additional safety precaution should you receive

a call indicating something has happened to myself or another family member, please take down the

information, ask the caller for a return telephone number and contact me at one of the numbers listed

below. If you cannot reach me, then the person to call in an emergency is _____
                                                                      (Name of Person)

_____ _____.
                            (Phone Number)

Additional Information: _____

_____

_____

You can reach me at the following numbers:

_____   _____
            (Work)   *(Cell Phone)*

_____   _____
            (Home)   *(Pager)*

Thank you for your assistance.

Sincerely,

_____

Attachment: Copy of Court Order

Children (continued)

Who has permission to remove my child (children) from Day Care?

Name: Driver's License Number: Physical Description:

_____   _____   _____
_____   _____   _____
_____   _____   _____
_____   _____   _____
_____   _____   _____
_____   _____   _____

Unauthorized Person: _____
                                          (Name)

_____ _____ _____ _____ _____
(Height)   *(Weight)*   *(Hair Color)*   *(Facial Hair)*   *(Other)*

The vehicle he/she drives is:

_____ _____ _____ _____ _____
(Make)   *(Model)*   *(Year)*   *(Color)*   *(License Plate)*

Other Information:

_____
_____
_____

It is not unusual for the alleged abuser to contact family and friends to find out where you are staying.

Instruct them not to give out any information-**no matter what.**

Give your family and friends this form (Form J) with a copy of your order of protection. Should the alleged abuser come around they are to contact the police immediately by calling 911 and explain that there is an order of protection in place and that they have a copy with them.

The abuser might go to a family member or friend's door who could unknowingly answer questions about you. Your friends or relatives may have no idea what this person looks like. It is imperative that you explain the gravity of the situation to them. Providing this form to them should keep them on their toes.

The abuser may also attempt to speak with neighbors or your landlord. Make sure you give them a copy of the form and your court order of protection.

It is important during this time that you connect with family and friends. Creating an emotional support system for both you and/or your children will lessen the stress of your situation.

Family & Friends *(Phone Number and Contact Sheet)*

Family & Friends

1) _____
   (Name)   *(Phone Number)*   *(Address, City, State, Zip)*

2) _____
   (Name)   *(Phone Number)*   *(Address, City, State, Zip)*

3) _____
   (Name)   *(Phone Number)*   *(Address, City, State, Zip)*

4) _____
   (Name)   *(Phone Number)*   *(Address, City, State, Zip)*

5) _____
   (Name)   *(Phone Number)*   *(Address, City, State, Zip)*

6) _____
   (Name)   *(Phone Number)*   *(Address, City, State, Zip)*

7) _____
   (Name)   *(Phone Number)*   *(Address, City, State, Zip)*

8) _____
   (Name)   *(Phone Number)*   *(Address, City, State, Zip)*

9) _____
   (Name)   *(Phone Number)*   *(Address, City, State, Zip)*

10) _____
   (Name)   *(Phone Number)*   *(Address, City, State, Zip)*

11) _____
   (Name)   *(Phone Number)*   *(Address, City, State, Zip)*

12) _____
   (Name)   *(Phone Number)*   *(Address, City, State, Zip)*

13) _____
   (Name)   *(Phone Number)*   *(Address, City, State, Zip)*

14) _____
   (Name)   *(Phone Number)*   *(Address, City, State, Zip)*

15) _____
   (Name)   *(Phone Number)*   *(Address, City, State, Zip)*

16) _____
   (Name)   *(Phone Number)*   *(Address, City, State, Zip)*

YOU MAY USE THIS FORM TO NOTIFY YOUR FAMILY AND FRIENDS.

Date: _____

To: _____

Address: _____

City, State, Zip: _____

Dear: _____

Attach a Recent Photo

Attached is a recent photo of _____ with whom I have ended a relationship. My situation at the present time is very serious and right now my safety, and that of my children, is first and foremost. Please know that I/we are safe. I have taken the necessary legal steps to move forward with my life. If you receive calls alleging something has happened to either me or the kids, remain calm, take down the information and immediately contact the following person(s) (i.e. name of lawyer, police, and other telephone numbers). Please do not disclose that you received this letter from me.

_____

_____

Be careful not to give information about me to anyone. I will contact you when things settle down. The description of the person is as follows:

_____	_____	_____	_____	_____
(Height)	*(Weight)*	*(Hair Color)*	*(Facial Hair)*	*(Other)*

The vehicle he/she drives is:

_____	_____	_____	_____	_____
(Make)	*(Model)*	*(Year)*	*(Color)*	*(License Plate)*

Additional comments: _____

_____

Sincerely,

_____

Attachment: Copy of Court Order

Your Employer

Your personal safety at work is very important. You must be thinking that you cannot tell anyone because you are afraid you will lose your job, that it is not important, or that it is no one's business. By thinking this way you not only place yourself in harms way, but also those with whom you work. Example: You had your husband served divorce papers or an order of protection while you were at work. He's angry and wants to confront you about this. The first place he will come is your workplace. He could be waiting in the company parking lot for you or maybe the receptionist, who knows him, allows him to enter the office. Maybe he is so angry he has a weapon and is going to threaten you with bodily harm if you do not go with him to talk or do as he demands. Additionally, you could be caught off guard when someone tells you that there has been an accident with a family member. You react by grabbing your keys and running out the door. The only accident is that you have been duped into leaving the building so your husband or boyfriend can confront you and possibly hurt you.

Here Are a Few Tips for Office Safety:

* Don't leave your employer in the dark. It is their business. If you have a human resource department or employee handbook, check to see if your employer offers assistance in these situations.
* Alert your employer that you have an order of protection.
* Give this form (Form K), with a recent picture of your abuser and a copy of the court order, to someone who can assist you at your place of business. Ask that all phone calls be screened or transferred temporarily to another person until things settle down. If there is a security guard on-site, or a company that patrols the grounds, make sure they also receive a copy of both the order of protection and the employer form (Form K).
* Don't allow deliveries of any kind-not even flowers-to come to you directly.
* If you work in a public place, ask that you be reassigned.
* Change your work schedule if possible.
* Park your car in a secure, well-lighted area and always ask someone to see you to your vehicle safely. Have your car keys ready in your hand.
* It is your responsibility to report all phone calls and incidents to the police while your order of protection is in effect.
* Keep a log of all threatening phone calls.
* Follow-up with the Attorney's Office who helped you obtain the court order and let them know what is happening.
* Always carry your order of protection and a photo of him at all times.

YOU MAY USE THIS FORM TO NOTIFY YOUR EMPLOYER.

Date: _____

To: _____
                    (Name of Employer)

Address: _____

City, State, Zip: _____

```
┌─────────────────┐
│                 │
│                 │
│                 │
│   Attach a      │
│   Recent Photo  │
│                 │
│                 │
│                 │
│                 │
└─────────────────┘
```

Dear: _____

My name is _____ and I work in _____

My company telephone number is _____. I recently have ended my relationship

with _____ attached is a recent photo. His/her name is

_____. The description of the person is as follows:

_____	_____	_____	_____	_____
(Height)	*(Weight)*	*(Hair Color)*	*(Facial Hair)*	*(Other)*

The vehicle he/she drives is:

_____	_____	_____	_____	_____
(Make)	*(Model)*	*(Year)*	*(Color)*	*(License Plate)*

If this person calls or shows up at the company, please contact the police immediately. I have also

attached a copy of my court order of protection that prohibits the person from calling and/or coming to

the workplace.

Other remarks: _____

_____

As an additional safety precaution, should someone call and say it's an "emergency" i.e., something
happened to a family member, the call should not be transferred to me. Instead please take a written
message.

Thank you for your assistance,

Sincerely,

_____

Attachment: Copy of Court Order

Often, landlords or apartment complex managers are very understanding once they are given information regarding potential situations that may arise. Make an appointment with the landlord or whomever handles property rentals. If you can, bring along a recent photo of the abuser, the order of protection if one has been issued by the courts, and the letter on page 119.

You need to give your landlord this form (Form L), along with a recent photo of the abuser, and make sure someone on your property has a copy of this form along with a copy of an order of protection (if you have received one).

The landlord or management of the building where you live may, or may not, have ever seen the abuser. This might be an embarrassing situation, but you must think of your safety and the safety of those around you.

Preparing the person you rent from will allow a safer living environment for you and your neighbors.

Renting *(Phone Number and Contact Sheet)*

_____   _____   Given copy on: _____
(Name of Contact Person)   (Phone Number)

Remarks: _____

_____

_____   _____   Given copy on: _____
(Name of Contact Person)   (Phone Number)

Remarks: _____

_____

_____   _____   Given copy on: _____
(Name of Contact Person)   (Phone Number)

Remarks: _____

_____

_____   _____   Given copy on: _____
(Name of Contact Person)   (Phone Number)

Remarks: _____

_____

_____   _____   Given copy on: _____
(Name of Contact Person)   (Phone Number)

Remarks: _____

_____

_____   _____   Given copy on: _____
(Name of Contact Person)   (Phone Number)

Remarks: _____

_____

Renting

*YOU MAY USE THIS FORM TO NOTIFY YOUR BUILDING MANAGEMENT COMPANY, PROPERTY MANAGER OR LANDLORD IN THE CASE OF AN **ABUSIVE** RELATIONSHIP.*

Date: _____

To: _____
      (Name of building management company, property manager, landlord)

Address: _____

City, State, Zip:_____

TO WHOM IT MAY CONCERN:

My name is _____and I live at the following address:

_____.

On _____, I spoke with _____ from your office.
          (Date)

I am writing this letter to confirm the information which I have already conveyed. I am concerned for my

personal safety and the safety of my children. You are hereby placed on notice that this information is to

remain completely confidential and that under no circumstances is this information to be released to any

one without a Certified Court Order or without providing the following password _____ to

you.

Please direct all communications, including billing and inquiries to the following address:

_____

_____

You can reach me at the following numbers:

_____	_____
(Work)	*(Cell Phone)*
_____	_____
(Home)	*(Pager)*

Thank you in advance for your assistance.

Sincerely,

_____

YOU MAY USE THIS FORM TO NOTIFY YOUR BUILDING MANAGEMENT COMPANY, PROPERTY MANAGER OR LANDLORD IN THE CASE OF A **NON-ABUSIVE** RELATIONSHIP.

Date: _____

To: _____
   (Name of building management company, property manager, landlord)

Address: _____

City, State, Zip:_____

TO WHOM IT MAY CONCERN:

My name is _____ and I live at the following address:

_____.

On _____, I spoke with _____ from your office.
   (Date)
Please have your records changed to reflect the following:_____

_____

_____

_____

As an additional safety precaution, please place the following password _____ on all

information. Due to personal reasons, under no circumstances is information to be released to anyone,

without first providing you with the password. Please direct all communications, including billing and

inquiries to the following address:_____

_____

You can reach me at the following numbers:

_____   _____
             (Work)   *(Cell Phone)*

_____   _____
             (Home)   *(Pager)*

Thank you in advance for your assistance.

Sincerely,

_____

You may receive social security, disability, or some other form of income on a monthly basis. This form (Form N) will allow you to continue to receive your checks at a new location without interruption.

Abusers can be clever and often think of ways to make your life miserable. One way is to see that you don't get your checks directly.

It is a good idea to have this form notarized at a currency exchange and to sign this form in front of the notary so that he can witness your signature on the document.

Make sure to make copies and send them registered mail with a return receipt requested. Call back in a week to make sure this information was put into the system.

Staple or clip a copy of all returned receipts to this page.

Social Service Agency *(Phone Number and Contact Sheet)*

_____   _____   _____
(Name of Agency)   *(Contact Person)*   *(Phone Number)*

Remarks: _____

_____

_____   _____   _____
(Name of Agency)   *(Contact Person)*   *(Phone Number)*

Remarks: _____

_____

_____   _____   _____
(Name of Agency)   *(Contact Person)*   *(Phone Number)*

Remarks: _____

_____

_____   _____   _____
(Name of Agency)   *(Contact Person)*   *(Phone Number)*

Remarks: _____

_____

_____   _____   _____
(Name of Agency)   *(Contact Person)*   *(Phone Number)*

Remarks: _____

_____

_____   _____   _____
(Name of Agency)   *(Contact Person)*   *(Phone Number)*

Remarks: _____

_____

YOU MAY USE THIS FORM TO NOTIFY WELFARE AND SOCIAL SERVICE AGENCIES.

Date _____

To: _____
(Name of Agency)

From:_____

Address:_____

Social Security No.:_____

City, State, Zip:
_____

Date of Birth:
_____

TO WHOM IT MAY CONCERN:

My name is _____ and I am currently receiving

assistance from your agency. The check is currently being mailed to _____
(Former Address)

_____.

I am requesting that all checks and inquiries be sent to the following address: _____

_____
(New Address)

to the attention of _____. As an additional safety precaution, please
(Person's Name)

place the following password _____ on all information. Due to personal reasons that

involve my safety, under no circumstances is information to be released to anyone, without first providing

you with the password. If your office needs to communicate with me, either do so at my new mailing

address or leave a message at _____.
(Telephone Number)

Thank your in advance for your assistance.

Sincerely,

_____

Knowing where to locate resources can be frustrating and time consuming. In this section, we have compiled information from child support enforcement, child custody and child protection agencies, and parental kidnapping resources.

For a listing of battered women's shelters, either contact the National Coalition Against Domestic Violence (listed here) or go to your local yellow pages, under Women's Organizations or Social Services, for information.

Like our fingerprints, no two situations are the same. It is important that you plan and chart out a course of action, not just for your safety, but also for peace of mind. There are many wonderful organizations and resources across the country. Unfortunately,there isn't room to list them all. Look in your local phone book, go to your local library, or begin contacting those provided in this guide.

CHILDFIND OF AMERICA
A network of individuals and groups serving as a contact point for separated children and parents; also publishes a newsletter.
Phone: 800.426.5678

CHILDREN OF THE NIGHT
14530 Sylvan Street, Van Nuys, CA 91441
Phone: 818.908.4474
Fax: 818.908.1468

CLEARINGHOUSE OF CHILD ABUSE AND NEGLECT INFORMATION
Provides information and publishes materials.
Phone: 800.394.3366
Website: www.nccanch.acf.hhs.gov

FIND THE CHILDREN
11811 W. Olympic Boulevard, Los Angeles, CA 90064
Phone: 310.477.6721
Fax: 310.477.7166

INTERSTATE ASSOCIATION FOR STOLEN CHILDREN
10033 Yukon River Way, Rancho Cordova, CA 95670-2725
Phone: 916.631.7631
Fax: 916.631.1009
E-mail: iasckids@pacbell.net
Website: www.members.aol.com/iasc4kids/index.html

NATIONAL CENTER FOR MISSING AND EXPLOITED CHILDREN
A clearinghouse for parents searching for missing children.
Phone: 800.843.5678

NATIONAL COUNCIL ON CHILD ABUSE AND FAMILY VIOLENCE
Provides referrals to related agencies and shelters, as well as pamphlets on the various aspects of child abuse and family violence.
Phone: 800.222.2000
Website: www.nccafv.org

NATIONAL RESOURCE CENTER ON CHILD ABUSE AND NEGLECT
Provides information and referrals to local services.
Phone: 800.227.5242

THE PAUL AND LISA PROGRAM
P.O. Box 348, Westbrook, CT 06498
Phone: 860.767.7660
Fax: 303.792.9900

VANISHED CHILDREN'S ALLIANCE
Complete services and help with foreign languages: Spanish, Filipino, Greek, Lao, Cambodian, Chinese, and Arabic. Expert witnesses available. 2095 Park Avenue, San Jose, CA 95125
Phone: 408.296.1113
Fax: 408.296.1117
Sightings only: 800.826.4743
Website: www.fga.com/vanished

Personal Record

FORM	DATE MAILED	DATE PHONED	SPOKE WITH (name)
A: Car Insurance			
B: Utilities			
B: Utilities			
B: Utilities			
B: Utilities			
B: Utilities			
C: Financial			
D: Accountant			
E: Medical			
E: Medical			
E: Medical			
E: Medical			
E: Medical			
F: Credit Card Companies			
F: Credit Card Companies			
F: Credit Card Companies			
F: Credit Card Companies			
F: Credit Card Companies			
F: Credit Card Companies			
G: Credit Report Request			

ABUSIVE RELATIONSHIP FORMS:

FORM	DATE MAILED	DATE PHONED	SPOKE WITH (name)
H: Police/States Attorney			
I: Children			
J: Family/Friends			
J: Family/Friends			
J: Family/Friends			
J: Family/Friends			
J: Family/Friends			
K: Employer			
L: Home/Abusive			
M: Home/Non-Abusive			
N: Social Service Agency			

*KEEP A COPY OF ALL FORMS YOU SEND IN A SAFE LOCATION. DO NOT WRITE PASSWORDS ON THIS SHEET.

Notes:

Notes:

Notes:

Notes:

ABA OFFICE - ALABAMA
P.O. Box 671, Montgomery, AL 36101
Phone: 334.269.1515
Website: www.alabar.org

ABA OFFICE - ALASKA
P.O. Box 100279, Anchorage, AK 99511
Phone: 907.272.0352
Website: www.alaskabar.org

ABA OFFICE - ARIZONA
111 West Monroe, Suite 1800, Phoenix, AZ 85003
Phone: 602.252.4804
Website: www.azbar.org

ABA OFFICE - ARKANSAS
400 W. Markham St., Little Rock, AR 72201
Phone: 501.375.4605
Website: www.arkbar.com

ABA OFFICE - CALIFORNIA
1149 South Hill St., Los Angeles, CA 90015
Phone: 213.765.1000
Website: www.calbar.org

ABA OFFICE - COLORADO
1900 Grant Street, Suite 950, Denver, CO 80203
Phone: 303.860.1115
Website: www.cobar.org

ABA OFFICE - CONNECTICUT
30 Bank Street, P.O. Box 350, New Britain, CT 06050-0350
Phone: 860.223.4400
Website: www.ctbar.org

ABA OFFICE - DELAWARE
1201 Orange Street, Wilmington, DE 19801
Phone: 302.658.5279
Website: www.dsba.org

ABA OFFICE - DISTRICT OF COLUMBIA
1250 H St., N.W., Washington, DC 20005
Phone: 202.737.4700
Website: www.dcbar.org

ABA OFFICE - FLORIDA
650 Appalachia Pkwy., Tallahassee, FL 32399-3200
Phone: 850.561.5600
Website: www.flabar.org

ABA OFFICE - GEORGIA
800 The Hurt Bldg., 50 Hurt Plaza, Atlanta, GA 30303
Phone: 404.527.8700
Website: www.gabar.org

ABA OFFICE - HAWAII
1132 Bishop, Suite 906, Honolulu, HI 96813
Phone: 808.537.1868
Website: www.hsba.org

ABA OFFICE - IDAHO
525 W. Jefferson St., Boise, ID 83701
Phone: 208.334.4500
Website: www.state.id.us/isb

ABA OFFICE - ILLINOIS
424 S. Second St., Springfield, IL 62701
Phone: 217.525.1760
Website: www.illinoisbar.org

ABA OFFICE - INDIANA
230 East Ohio St., 4th Floor Indianapolis, IN 46204
Phone: 317.639.5465
Website: www.inbar.org

ABA OFFICE - IOWA
521 E. Locust St., Suite 300
Des Moines, IA 50309-1939
Phone: 515.243.3179
Website: www.iowabar.org

ABA OFFICE - KANSAS
1200 SW Harrison, Topeka, KS 66601-1037
Phone: 785.234.5696
Website: www.ksbar.org

ABA OFFICE - KENTUCKY
514 W. Main St., Frankfort, KY 40601
Phone: 502.564.3795
Website: www.kybar.org

ABA OFFICE - LOUISIANA
601 St. Charles Ave., New Orleans, LA 70130
Phone: 504.566.1600
Website: www.lsba.org

ABA OFFICE - MAINE
124 State St., P.O. Box 788, Augusta, ME 04332
Phone: 207.622.7523
Website: www.mainebar.org

ABA OFFICE - MARYLAND
520 West Sayette St., Baltimore, MD 21201
Phone: 410.685.7878
Website: www.msba.org

ABA OFFICE - MASSACHUSETTS
20 West St., Boston, MA 02111
Phone: 617.542.3602
Website: www.massbar.org

ABA OFFICE - MICHIGAN
306 Townsend St., Lansing, MI 48933
Phone: 517.372.9030
Website: www.michbar.org

ABA OFFICE - MINNESOTA
600 Nicolette Mall, Suite 380, Minneapolis, MN 55402
Phone: 612.333.1183
Website: www.mnbar.org

ABA OFFICE - MISSISSIPPI
P.O. Box 2168, Jackson, MS 39225-2168
Phone: 601.948.4471
Website: www.msbar.org

ABA OFFICE - MISSOURI
326 Monroe St., Jefferson City, MO 65101
Phone: 573.635.4128
Website: www.mobar.org

ABA OFFICE - MONTANA
P.O. Box 577, Helena, MT 59624
Phone: 406.442.7660
Website: www.montanabar.org

ABA OFFICE - NEBRASKA
635 South 14th St., Lincoln, NE 68501
Phone: 402.475.7091
Website: www.nebar.com

ABA OFFICE - NEVADA
600 East Charleston, Las Vegas, NV 89104
Phone: 775.329.4100
Website: www.nvbar.org

ABA OFFICE - NEW HAMPSHIRE
112 Pleasant St., Concord, NH 03301
Phone: 603.224.6942
Website: www.nhbar.org

ABA OFFICE - NEW JERSEY
1 Constitution Square, New Brunswick, NJ 08901
Phone: 732.249.5000
Website: www.njsba.com

ABA OFFICE - NEW MEXICO
P.O. Box 25883, Albuquerque, NM 87125
Phone: 505.797.6000
Website: www.nmbar.org

ABA OFFICE - NEW YORK
One Elk St., Albany, NY 12207
Phone: 518.463.3200
Website: www.nysba.org

ABA OFFICE - NORTH CAROLINA
P.O. Box 25908, Raleigh, NC 27611
Phone: 919.828.4620
Website: www.ncbar.com

ABA OFFICE - NORTH DAKOTA
515½ East Broadway, Bismarck, ND 58502-0530
Phone: 800.472.2685
Website: www.sband.org

Resources *(Alphabetical Listing)*

ABA OFFICE - OHIO
1700 Lake Shore Dr., P.O. Box 16562
Columbus, OH 43216-16562
Phone: 614.487.2050
Website: www.ohiobar.org

ABA OFFICE - OKLAHOMA
P.O. Box 53036, Oklahoma City, OK 73152
Phone: 405.524.2365
Website: www.okbar.org

ABA OFFICE - OREGON
P.O. Box 1689, Lake Oswego, OR 97035
Phone: 503.620.0222
Website: www.osbar.org

ABA OFFICE - PENNSYLVANIA
100 South St., P.O. Box 186
Harrisburg, PA 17108
Phone: 717.238.6715
Website: www.pabar.org

ABA OFFICE - RHODE ISLAND
115 Cedar St., Providence, RI 02903
Phone: 401.421.5740
Website: www.ribar.com

ABA OFFICE - SOUTH CAROLINA
P.O. Box 608, Columbia, SC 29292.0608
Phone: 803.799.6653
Website: www.scbar.org

ABA OFFICE - SOUTH DAKOTA
222 East Capitol Ave., Pierre, SD 57501
Phone: 605.224.7554
Website: www.sdbar.org

ABA OFFICE - TENNESSEE
3622 West End Ave., Nashville, TN 37205
Phone: 615.383.7421
Website: www.tba.org

ABA OFFICE - TEXAS
P.O. Box 12487, Austin, TX 78711
Phone: 512.463.1463
Website: www.texasbar.com

ABA OFFICE - UTAH
654 S. 200 East St., Salt Lake City, UT 84111
Phone: 801.531.9110
Website: www.utahbar.org

ABA OFFICE - VERMONT
P.O. Box 100, Montpelier, VT 05601
Phone: 802.223.2020
Website: www.vtbar.org

ABA OFFICE - VIRGINIA
707 East Main St., Suite 1500, Richmond, VA 23219-2803
Phone: 804.775.0500
Website: www.vsb.org

ABA OFFICE - WASHINGTON
2104 4th Ave., 4th Floor, Seattle, WA 90121
Phone: 206.727.8200
Website: www.wsba.org

ABA OFFICE - WEST VIRGINIA
2006 Kanawha Blvd. East, Charleston, WV 25311
Phone: 304.558.2456
Website: www.wvbar.org

ABA OFFICE - WISCONSIN
P.O. Box 7158, Madison, WI 53707-7158
Phone: 608.257.3838
Website: www.wisbar.org

ABA OFFICE - WYOMING
P.O. Box 109, Cheyenne, WY 82003
Phone: 307.632.9061
Website: www.wyomingbar.org

AGENCY FOR HEALTH CARE POLICY AND RESEARCH CLEARINGHOUSE

A free guide titled: *Prescription Medicines and You*, is available.
Phone: 800.358.9295
Website: www.ahcpr.gov/consumer/ncpiebro.htm

ALCOHOLICS ANONYMOUS

A network of mutual support groups for recovering alcoholics. See your local telephone White Pages for local groups.
Phone: 212.870.3400

AMERICANS WITH DISABILITIES INFORMATION LINE

U.S. Department of Justice
Phone: 800.514.0301 TDD: 800.514.0383
Website: www.usdoj.gov/crt/ada/infoline.htm

APPLYING FOR A LOAN

On-line lenders that can pre-qualify for loans.
Website: www.eloan.com
Website: www.mortgage.com
Website: www.loanworks.com
Website: www.quicken.com

Visit this site to have an idea of what you would be paying on a monthly mortgage. Also explains how to obtain and understand your credit report and the different types of mortgages that are available.
Website: www.Interest.com

AUTO

Contains free advice about car repairs, how to find a reputable mechanic etc.
Website: www.my-auto-mechanic.com

BREAST HEALTH ACCESS FOR WOMEN WITH DISABILITIES

Offers breast health information, screenings and early Breast Cancer detection.
Phone: 510.204.4866 TDD: 510.204.4574
Website: www.bhawd.org/sitefiles/index2.html

BUDGET PLANNING

Assists you with budgeting, planning, and spending.
Website: www.mybudgetplanner.com

CENTER FOR DISEASE CONTROL - NATIONAL IMMUNIZATION PROGRAM

Phone: 800.232.0233 Website: www.cdc.gov
Spanish Immunization hotline: 800.232.0233
English Immunization hotline: 800.CDC.SHOT

CENTER FOR DISEASE - NATIONAL AIDS HOTLINE

Phone: 800.342.AIDS (English)
800.344.7432 (Spanish) TDD: 800.243.7889

CENTER FOR DISEASE - NATIONAL AIDS CLEARINGHOUSE

Phone: 800.458.5231 TDD: 800.243.7012
Website: www.cdcnpin.org

CENTERS FOR INDEPENDENT LIVING

An information site for people with disabilites.
Website: www.ilusa.com

CHILDFIND OF AMERICA

A network of individuals and groups serving as a contact point for separated children and parents; also publishes a newsletter.
Phone: 800.426.5678

CHILDREN OF THE NIGHT

14530 Sylvan Street, Van Nuys, CA 91441
Phone: 818.908.4474
Fax: 818.908.1468

CHILD SUPPORT ENFORCEMENT ABROAD

This site offers step-by-step guidance, general information, and reference resources from the U.S. State Department. This is a good site for parents and lawyers trying to enforce child support when the person required to make payments has left the country.
Website: www.travel.state.gov/family/child-support.html

CLEARINGHOUSE OF CHILD ABUSE AND NEGLECT INFORMATION

Provides information and publishes materials.
Phone: 800.394.3366
Website: www.nccanch.acf.hhs.gov

COLLEGE BOARD CONTACT INFORMATION

This site has a wealth of information about the
College Board's resources.
Website: www.collegeboard.org

COLLEGE CREDIT EDUCATION LOAN PROGRAM

Students interested in applying for College Credit
Education Loans should call 800.832.5626 or contact
their aid administrators. For additional information
about College Credit, contact: Jennifer Jenkins,
Manager; College Credit Education Loan Program;
The College Board: 11911 Freedom Drive, Suite
400, Reston, VA 20190
Phone: 800.626.9795 or 703.707.8999
Fax: 708.707.5599
E-mail: CollegeCredit@collegeboard.org

CONSUMER CREDIT COUNSELING

Non-profit organization providing NO CHARGE
assistance to those needing help with budgeting
monthly bills, credit card debt, or facing foreclosure.
Website: www.cccs.org

CONSUMER PROTECTION

Sites that teach you how to manage and remove
information.
www.cookiecentral.com/c_concept.htm

This site is maintained by the Federal Trade
Commission and offers buyers guides, tips, and links
to other useful resources.
Website: www.consumer.gov

CSS/FINANCIAL AID PROFILE

Students with questions or comments about PRO-
FILE should call CSS at 305.829.9793 from 8 am to
10 pm, Eastern Time, Sunday through Friday, from
September 15 to April 1. After April 1, service hours
are 8 am to 6 pm. Eastern Time, Monday through
Friday, and are subject to change.

Financial aid administrators or high school coun-
selors with questions and comments about PROFILE
should contact one of the CSS Regional Offices.
Also call to order additional copies of the PROFILE
Registration Guide or the PROFILE Basic
Application.
Phone: 800.239.5888. TDD: 800.915.9990
E-mail: help@cssprofile.org

FIND THE CHILDREN

11811 W. Olympic Boulevard, Los Angeles, CA
90064
Phone: 310.477.6721
Fax: 310.477.7166

DEPARTMENT OF MOTOR VEHICLES

Offices are located in every state and usually in
every county seat municipality. Each state has different regulations about the information they will
release to an individual. The police working on your
case will probably be able to access the records more
easily, once criminal charges have been filed.

DIVORCE SOURCE

This interactive site includes discussion forums pertaining to divorce issues, including custody and visitation, parental abduction, and domestic violence.
This site also features helpful resource services and
books that might be of assistance.
Website: www.divorcesource.com

FANNIE MAE CONSUMER RESOURCE CENTER

Phone: 800.732.6643
Website: www.fanniemae.com

FEDERAL CITIZEN INFORMATION CENTER

Phone: 800.FED.INFO
TDD: 800.326.2996 (hearing-impaired)

FEDERAL GOVERNMENT INFORMATION LINE

You can gain information on how to request information under the Federal Freedom of Information Act.
Phone: 800.688.9889

FEDERAL STUDENT AID INFORMATION CENTER
Phone: 800.4.FED.AID (1.800.433.3243)

FINANCIAL
An on-line financial resource for single moms.
Website: www.making-ends-meet.org

FOOD STAMP PROGRAM
Provides information on how to apply for food stamps. Also directs people who would like to help friends or relatives acquire food stamps.
Website: www.fns.usda.gov/fsp/

GOVERNMENT RESOURCES
This government guide, available on-line, offers welfare and low income assistance, and child support information that includes enforcement. This site also includes food stamps, health insurance, housing and heating assistance, legal aid, senior services, and information on domestic violence.
Website: governmentguide.com/benefits/welfare

HEALTH FINDER
A website service created by the U.S. Department of Health and Human Services offering information on health care, health information links and an A to Z online library.
Website: http://www.healthfinder.gov/

HEALTH INSURANCE
Low cost health insurance for children.
Website: www.insurekidsnow.gov

INSURANCE QUOTES
Quotesmith maintains a database of approximately 350 health insurance companies across the country. This service allows you to get instant quotes for life, medical, auto, and dental insurance as well as Medicare supplements if you are age 65 or over. If you do not have a computer, you can call them at 800.556.9393,
7 am to 10 pm Monday through Friday, and 8 am to 5 pm Saturday (Central time).
Website: www.quotesmith.com

INTERNET SAFETY
A resource for parents offering Internet safety tips with links to filtering software.
Website: http://disney.go.com/cybersafety/

INTERNET LEGAL RESOURCE GUIDE
This site offers: basic agreements, buying and selling, credit and collection, employment, leases and tenancies, loans and borrowing, personal and family, transfers and assignments, business and much, much more.
Website: www.ilrg.com

INTERSTATE ASSOCIATION FOR STOLEN CHILDREN
10033 Yukon River Way, Rancho Cordova, CA 95670-2725
Phone: 916.631.7631
Fax: 916.631.1009
E-mail: iasckids@pacbell.net
Website:
www.members.aol.com/iasc4kids/index.html

JOB OPPORTUNITIES
Job opportunities for low income people
Website: www.govbenefits.gov/index.jsp

Assists you with resumes, computer skills, employment services, and a GED diploma
Website: www.transform-me.org

LEGAL
State-by-State legal resources for domestic violence victims
Website: www.womenslaw.org

Listing of State- by-State Child Support Enforcement
Website: www.divorcenet.com

Dedicated in getting unpaid court ordered child support
Website: www.wantedposters.com

Resources for unpaid child support in Canada
Website: www.Fadcanada.org

Helps parents get child support
Website: www.nationalchildsupport.com

NATIONAL CENTER FOR MISSING AND EXPLOITED CHILDREN

A clearinghouse for parents searching for missing children.
Phone: 800.843.5678

NATIONAL CLEARINGHOUSE FOR ALCOHOL AND DRUG INFORMATION

Focuses on preventive and health-related info.
Phone: 800.729.6686
Website: www.health.org

NATIONAL COALITION AGAINST DOMESTIC VIOLENCE

Provides information on battered women's shelters in your area, 24 hours a day 7 days a week.
National Hotline: 800.799.7233
TDD: 800.787.3224

NATIONAL COUNCIL ON CHILD ABUSE AND FAMILY VIOLENCE

Provides referrals to related agencies and shelters, as well as pamphlets on the various aspects of child abuse and family violence.
Phone: 800.222.2000
Website: www.nccafv.org

NATIONAL DAYCARE REFERRAL AGENCY

For assistance in finding quality daycare and referral
Phone: 800.424.2246

THE NATIONAL DRUG INFORMATION, TREATMENT AND REFERRAL LINE

Free and confidential. The hours are 9 am-3 am (Monday-Friday) and 12 noon-3 am (Saturday-Sunday).
Phone: 800.662.HELP or 800.66.AYUDA (Spanish)
Website: www.drughelp.org

NATIONAL HEADACHE FOUNDATION

A good resource with information on the latest in headache causes and treatments. Includes self management tips to minimize the impact of headaches in your life.
Phone: 888.NHF.5552
Website: www.headaches.org

NATIONAL ORGANIZATION FOR VICTIM ASSISTANCE

Publishes a newsletter, NOVA, and maintains a national directory of services for victims of all types.
Phone: 800.879.6682
Website: www.try-nova.org

NATIONAL RESOURCE CENTER ON CHILD ABUSE AND NEGLECT

Provides information and referrals to local services.
Phone: 800.227.5242

NATIONAL RUNAWAY SWITCHBOARD

Phone: 800.621.4000 TDD: 800.621.0394
Website: www.nrscrisline.org

NATIONAL WOMEN'S HEALTH INFORMATION CENTER

Provides a free, reliable health information to women everywhere.
Phone: 800.994.9662
Website: www.4women.gov

Women with Disabilities web page
Website: www.4woman.gov/wwd

OFFICE OF CITIZENSHIP, APPEALS AND LEGAL ASSISTANCE

1425 K Street, NW Rm. 300
Washington, D.C. 20522
Phone: 202.326.6168

OFFICE OF PERSONNEL MANAGEMENT

Can locate retired or active civil service or military personnel.
1900 E. Street, NW, Washington, D.C. 20415
Phone: 202.606.2424

PARENTS GUIDE TO THE INTERNET
Interactive site for both kids and parents.
Website: www.ed.gov/pubs/parents/internet/sites.html

THE PAUL AND LISA PROGRAM
P.O. Box 348, Westbrook, CT 06498
Phone: 860.767.7660
Fax: 303.792.9900

PERSONAL CREDIT CHECK
EXPERIAN (TRW), P.O. Box 2104, Allen, TX 75013
Phone: 800.EXPERIAN

EQUIFAX
800.685.1111(cost if $3-8 for a report)
Website: www.equifax.com

TRANS UNION
P.O. Box 7000, North Olmstead, Ohio 44070
Phone: 800.916.8800
Website: www.transunion.com

REGISTERED SEX OFFENDER REGISTRY
To find the registry pertinent to you, do an Internet search for "*Your State*" Sex Offender Registry. Click into the site and follow directions. A wealth of information is also available on the site below.
Website: www.sexcriminals.com

SALVATION ARMY
They provide emergency lodging, food, and shelter across America. See your Yellow Pages for the nearest location. Or you can write: Post Office Box 269, Alexandria, VA 22313

SCHOLARSHIPS AND FINANCIAL AID SOURCES ON THE INTERNET
This site contains information regarding general scholarships, universities, and colleges.
Website:
www.uscsu.sc.edu/student_affairs/scholar.htm

SCHOLARSHIPS AND SEARCH SERVICES
Financial aid offers from colleges are not the only source of assistance available to students. Millions of dollars are given away each year to deserving students by private organizations. Finding these scholarships and applying for them can be a frustrating, but rewarding process.

The best place to start looking for scholarships is in your high school guidance office. Once you have a handle on what is available locally, it is time to use the free scholarship search services available on the Internet.
Website: www.theoldschool.org/scholars.asp

SERVICE ACADEMIES

UNITED STATES AIR FORCE ACADEMY
Colorado Springs, CO 80840

UNITED STATES COAST GUARD ACADEMY
New London, CT 06320

UNITED STATES MERCHANT MARINE
Academy Kings Point, NY 10204

UNITED STATES MILITARY ACADEMY
West Point, NY 10996

UNITED STATES NAVAL ACADEMY
Annapolis, MD 21402

SOCIAL SECURITY INFORMATION
Phone: 800.772.1213 TDD: 800.325.0778
Website: www.ssa.gov

VANISHED CHILDREN'S ALLIANCE
Complete services and help with foreign languages: Spanish, Filipino, Greek, Lao, Cambodian, Chinese, and Arabic. Expert witnesses available.
2095 Park Avenue, San Jose, CA 95125
Phone: 408.296.1113
Fax: 408.296.1117
Sightings only: 800.826.4743
Website: www.fga.com/vanished

By the time the God made woman, he was into the second week of working overtime.
An angel appeared and said, "Why are you spending so much time on this one?"
And God answered, "Have you seen my spec sheet on her? She has to be able to run on diet coke and left-overs, have a kiss that can cure anything from a scraped knee to a broken heart. She must heal herself when she is sick AND can work 18 hour days."

The angel then noticed something, and reaching out, touched the woman's cheek. "Oops, it looks like you have a leak in this model," the angel said, "I think you're trying to put too much into this one."

"That's not a leak," God corrected, "that's a tear. The tear is her way of expressing her joy, her sorrow, her pain, her disappointment, her love, her loneliness, her grief, and her pride. Woman is truly amazing.

Women have strengths that amaze men.
They bear hardships and carry burdens, but they hold happiness, love, and joy.
They smile when they want to scream.
They sing when they want to cry.
They cry when they are happy and laugh when they are nervous.
They fight for what they believe in.
They stand up to injustice.
They don't take 'no' for an answer when they believe there is a better solution.
They go without so others can have.
They go to the doctor with a frightened friend.
They love unconditionally.
They cry when their children excel and cheer when their friends get awards.
They are happy when they hear about a birth or a wedding.
Their hearts break when a friend dies.
They grieve at the loss of a family member, yet they are strong when they think there is no strength left.
They know that a hug and a kiss can help to heal a broken heart.
Women come in all sizes, in all colors and shapes.
They'll drive, fly, walk, run or e-mail you to show how much they care about you.
The heart of a woman is what makes the world keep turning!
They bring joy and hope.
They have compassion and ideals.
They give moral support to their family and friends.
Women have vital things to say and everything to give."
"Are there no flaws?" the angel said.
"Of course, because nothing can be perfect, each woman will have her unique flaws. But there's one they all have in common. I've tried to get it out of the model, but not even I can seem to fix it."

"What's that?"

"They all tend to forget their worth."

Author: Unknown

An Important Book For Women Who Want To Help Themselves

Defending Our Lives
Getting Away from Domestic Violence & Staying Safe
By Susan Murphy-Milano

With detailed, practical information, Murphy-Milano guides women through the process of protecting themselves from domestic violence and stalking. Defending Our Lives is a much needed resource in the struggle millions of women go through to protect themselves from domestic violence and stalking.

"A smart, step-by-step plan that hopefully will save lives. If you don't need it, give it as a gift."
                                    -Susan Estrich, author of Real Rape

This book is available at your local bookstore, or through most libraries. For more information visit our website at www.MovingOutMovingOn.com, or contact:

Kind Living Publishing, LLC
P.O. Box 1819, Janesville, WI 53547-1819
Email Us: kindlivingpress@aol.com
Phone: 1-888-232-3417

Do you have words of encouragement you would like to share? We would love to hear from you.

Please write us at:

Moving Out Moving On
P.O. Box 1819
Janesville, WI 53547-1819

www.movingoutmovingon.com

The Author

Susan Murphy-Milano became an advocate for battered women at the tender age of four. One night while her parents were fighting, she pulled the kitchen chair up to the telephone so she could call the operator for help. Her father, a Chicago police detective, was beating her mother's head against the iron bedpost.

Living in a constant war zone equipped Susan with the knowledge and skills to assist others. Her father, an alcoholic and abuser for many years, kept the family in constant fear of their lives on a daily basis. For most of her parents' married life, he threatened, "If you leave, I will find you; if I find you, I will kill you." On January 19, 1989, Susan's father followed through on his threat before killing himself. That very night, after Susan discovered their bodies, she vowed to change the way society viewed domestic violence. Susan has become one of the country's foremost experts in the area of domestic violence, stalking, workplace violence and self help.

In 1993, she was instrumental in the passage of the Illinois stalking law and has consistently argued for the rights of battered women and children, both through legislation and through national television appearances and print media. For many years she ran a national organization that met the individual needs of battered women. These women, without Susan's assistance, would not have been able to safely leave their abusive relationships and lead healthy, productive lives.

In 1996, Doubleday published *Defending Our Lives, Getting Away From Domestic Violence and Staying Safe*. This systematic book presented a comprehensive guide to the options available to victims of abuse as well as family and friends who wanted to help them.